What people are saying about

The Conscience of a Progressive

The Conscience of a Progressive is...essential reading in our current political moment. Steven Klees parses the foundational differences between conservative, liberal and progressive analysis, worldview and policy programs...This book is a substantive primer to ideas and programmatic distinctions that goes beyond horse-race political reporting. A valuable roadmap to the power of progressive thinking and policy.
Chuck Collins: Institute for Policy Studies, co-editor, Inequality. org, author, *Born on Third Base*

In these very troubling times Klees' book avoids merely cataloging crimes to smartly critique conservative and liberal perspectives and reflect on...positive contributions of progressives on many critical issues.
Michael Albert: Author of *Practical Utopia: Strategies for a Desirable Society* and co-founder *Z Magazine* and South End Press

Steven Klees has written an ambitious and fascinating book, his crisp and engaging words cover everything from debates around sexuality to economic justice, education and development. The "progressive" contrasts with the "conservative" by standing for a more equal and ecological society, and the "liberal" in arguing that structural alternatives are necessary. This book will attract attention and readers in an America where progressive and practical policy solutions are increasingly in demand.
Derek Wall: Author of *Economics Af*
Ruins and a Road to the Future and for
for the UK Green Party

Prof Klees' book is a must read for anyone interested in politics, economics, and education today. During the latter part of the twentieth century, in far too many countries we have witnessed an unconscionable and steady shift to the right by liberals and social democratic parties resulting in a neoliberal consensus. Prof Klees' critique from a progressive perspective is extremely timely as it contributes to a necessary strategic reflection on how to rebuild a truly progressive movement.

David Edwards: General Secretary, Education International, the global teachers union

Professor Steven Klees, through succinct and accessible prose, delivers, from the perspective of a progressive worldview, a lively commentary on the key issues of our time – education and socio-economic development but also climate change, healthcare, war, and more…His refreshing analysis comes at a time when it is most needed – a time when the dominant neoliberal discourse stifles the search for alternatives and remains largely unchallenged. A time when social development, the environment and reason face sustained assault and when the world lurches inexorably and dangerously toward ecological disasters and the barbarism of devastating wars. Klees lucidly unravels the basis for the global triple scourge of poverty, inequality, and discrimination and reveals the threads connecting class inequality with racism, sexism, heterosexism and ableism that make up the social fabric of the global order while suggesting much-needed alternatives. He brings to bear his considerable experience of 5 decades of professional life and his rich body of work spans 30 countries. This crucial book answers critical questions for anyone seeking progressive change. It is also a spur to new struggles – and to new possibilities.

Salim Vally: Professor, University of Johannesburg and Director, Center for Education Rights and Transformation, co-author of *Education, Economy and Society*

Steven Klees has written an important and well-argued case for a new left politics that draws on the best of the old. He draws on his deep and extensive knowledge of education, and therefore of the potential of human beings if given the resources and encouragement to realise this potential, to present an original perspective on what it means to be progressive in the US today. It's a book which should be published and published soon as the issue of political alternatives to the present chaos gets urgent!

Hilary Wainwright: Author of *A New Politics from the Left*, former member of the editorial board of the *New Left Review*, current editor of *Red Pepper*, and Fellow at the Transnational Institute

The Conscience of
a Progressive

The Conscience of
a Progressive

Steven Klees

Winchester, UK
Washington, USA

JOHN HUNT PUBLISHING

First published by Zero Books, 2020
Zero Books is an imprint of John Hunt Publishing Ltd., No. 3 East St., Alresford,
Hampshire SO24 9EE, UK
office@jhpbooks.com
www.johnhuntpublishing.com
www.zero-books.net

For distributor details and how to order please visit the 'Ordering' section on our website.

Text copyright: Steven Klees 2019

ISBN: 978 1 78904 496 6
978 1 78904 497 3 (ebook)
Library of Congress Control Number: 2019948449

A CIP catalogue record for this book is available from the British Library.

Design: Stuart Davies

UK: Printed and bound by CPI Group (UK) Ltd, Croydon, CR0 4YY
US: Printed and bound by Thomson-Shore, 7300 West Joy Road, Dexter, MI 48130

We operate a distinctive and ethical publishing philosophy in
all areas of our business, from our global network of authors to
production and worldwide distribution.

Contents

Acknowledgments   xii

1. Introduction   1
2. Education in the US   16
3. Education Internationally   30
4. Economics   41
5. Poverty and Inequality   52
6. International Development   60
7. Capitalism   79
8. Implications for Education   94
9. Intersections   100
        Gender   101
        Race and Ethnicity   105
        LGBT Issues   109
        Disability   113
10. Other Major Issues   118
        Health Care   118
        The Environment   123
        War and Violence   128
11. A Note on Research   135
12. Conclusions   141

About the Author   159
Notes   160
References   171
Index   187

For Susanne, Carolina, Marcos, Murilo, and Theo
with the hope for a more progressive future
for all of us

Acknowledgments

In some ways, this book has been a lifetime in the making, as my progressive views developed. I first thought of writing it after reading Paul Krugman's *The Conscience of a Liberal* and then going back and reading Barry Goldwater's *The Conscience of a Conservative*. I felt then and, even now, that, especially in the US, progressive views are too little heard.

I owe an intellectual debt to too many scholars, researchers, analysts, activists, writers, and journalists to mention. Many of them are cited herein. I have been especially inspired and influenced over many years by many progressive colleagues who work in the area of education and international development and by many political economists and others who have challenged societal structures that lead to inequality, marginalization, and deprivation.

I wish to thank John Hunt Publishing and Zero Books for believing in this book and bringing it to fruition. Most special thanks to my wife and partner, Susanne Clawson, artist and sociologist extraordinaire, for her lifetime of support, reading and commenting on my writings, including several drafts of this book!

Chapter 1

Introduction

Barry Goldwater, Senator from Arizona, wrote *The Conscience of a Conservative* in 1960. Paul Krugman, Nobel Prize-winning economist, wrote *The Conscience of a Liberal* in 2007. In 2017, Jeff Flake, current Senator from Arizona, wrote a "homage" to Goldwater and also called it *Conscience of a Conservative*. I don't identify as either a conservative or a liberal and am writing this book to put forth a different view, one I find not well-represented in the media and press, especially in the US. I think of myself as a progressive. For many years in US politics the label "progressive" was used as a synonym for liberal because liberal had become a dirty word. More recently, with the rise in popularity of Senator Bernie Sanders and others in the Democratic Party, the label "progressive" has come to mean something more. But more about a progressive view in a bit. Also, I am not famous like Goldwater, Flake, and Krugman. I was trained as an economist and have worked mostly in the field of education and international development, but more about me in a bit as well. Let's start by looking at conservatives and liberals.

Conservatives

Goldwater's book is a forerunner to Tea Party conservative Republican politics and could read as their manifesto. In 1960, when the book was written, the right-wing was not nearly as strong in the Republican Party or in the US as it is today, but it was still strong enough to get Goldwater the Republican presidential nomination in 1964. However, he lost to Lyndon Johnson in what most pundits describe as a landslide (Johnson got 60 percent of the popular vote and 90 percent of the Electoral College votes).

For Goldwater, conservatives see "politics as the art of achieving the maximum amount of freedom for individuals that is consistent with the maintenance of social order."[1] Goldwater emphasizes that the conservatives "first concern will always be: *Are we maximizing freedom*?"[2] The book then goes on to identify crucial issues, the conservative perspective on them, and the problems with a liberal view. Perhaps most important among them is the "principle of limited government."[3] Goldwater argues: "Throughout history, government has proved to be the chief instrument for thwarting man's [sic] liberty." In the 1960s, he was referring to the involvement of the federal government in anything that he felt should be left to the states according to his understanding of the US Constitution. This included Social Security and other New Deal programs, high taxation, the promotion of labor unions, the general setting of "standards of education, health, and safety,"[4] the regulation of business and agriculture, civil rights legislation, school integration and more. The only place Goldwater saw the need for more federal government was in counteracting the "Soviet menace."[5]

For Goldwater, our national government grew from what the framers/founders intended: "a servant with sharply limited powers into a master with virtually unlimited power."[6] He saw the "stifling omnipresence of government" as "evil."[7] To change this required a new approach to government:

> The turn will come when we entrust the conduct of our affairs to men who understand that their first duty as public officials is to divest themselves of the power they have been given. It will come when America, in hundreds of communities throughout the nation, decides to put the man in office who is pledged to enforce the Constitution and restore the Republic. Who will proclaim in a campaign speech: I have little interest in streamlining government or in making it more efficient, for I mean to reduce its size. I do not undertake to promote

welfare, for I propose to extend freedom. My aim is not to pass laws, but to repeal them. It is not to inaugurate new programs but to cancel old ones that do violence to the Constitution, or that have failed in their purpose, or that impose on the people an unwarranted financial burden. I will not attempt to discover whether legislation is "needed" before I have first determined if it is constitutionally permissible. And if I should later be attacked for neglecting my constituents' "interests," I shall reply that I was informed that their main interest is liberty and that in that cause I am doing the very best I can.[8]

These views didn't get him elected in 1964, but they play much better today. While Goldwater was somewhat extreme for his time, these views are no longer extreme. They were expressed by many of the Republican candidates for president in 2016, some of these views even by Donald Trump, although he is far from a Goldwater/Tea Party conservative. But more about Trump in a bit. I find these conservative views completely wrongheaded,[9] as I will discuss throughout the book, but let us turn to a liberal's critique of conservatives and their alternative vision.

Liberals

Krugman's book never calls conservatives "evil," but his substance comes close. Certainly, for him, they are completely wrong. First, a word about labels. Labels are always problematic, but we need to categorize and classify in order to converse. Nonetheless, it should always be remembered that labels are approximations, never perfect fits, and there is always blurring at the borders. In this case, there are many people who would identify themselves as "conservative" but reject many of Goldwater's and Tea Party's views.[10] Krugman distinguishes between the right-wing conservatives – who he calls "movement conservatives" – and other more moderate conservative positions. In fact, Krugman spends much of his book looking at the shift of Republicans from a more moderate position in the 1950s and 1960s to a more extreme right-wing one in the 1980s and after.

Krugman provides an excellent tour of twentieth-century US politics and economics from a liberal perspective. The short version of that tour begins briefly with the poverty and vast inequality of the late-nineteenth century's Gilded Age which eventually leads us into the Great Depression. The New Deal, World War II, and other factors (to be discussed) yielded a more equal and prosperous country. The book focuses on the US after World War II. For Krugman, the period from the end of the war through the 1950s was a sort of Golden Age – Krugman calls it the "Great Convergence." The distribution of income had become more equal. Conservative Republicans, with the advent of a moderate like Eisenhower, finally gave up their decades-long effort to reverse the programs of the New Deal. The differences between conservative Republicans and liberal Democrats became less clear, and there was much bipartisanship in Washington.

The unrest of the 1960s started to break that consensus apart. Krugman places particular emphasis on the consequences of the struggle for civil rights and the shift in Southern states from Democrat to Republican. The underlying racism of those opposed to the civil rights movement fueled the election of Ronald Reagan and subsequent Republicans and led, along with other factors, to a slew of bad right-wing Republican policies that brought us today back to the income inequality of the Gilded Age, a shaky economy, and stark battle lines between conservatives and liberals – what Krugman calls the "Great Divergence." Of course, this history is quite complex, but Krugman's book-length treatment provides considerable insight into it. I will talk more about this later.

Krugman spends much of the book attacking the policies put forth by right-wing conservative Republicans. While

Krugman doesn't call it this, theirs is the politics of negativity.

Conservatives today, and in 2007 when George Bush (the elder) was president and Krugman wrote his book, seemed to be following Goldwater's above precepts to repeal laws and cut programs and supports in almost all areas (except defense). They are against taxes, especially for the rich, against civil rights legislation (for racial and ethnic minorities and now gays), against health care legislation (cut Medicaid, privatize Medicare, and, more recently, repeal Obamacare), against Social Security (again, privatize), against meaningful immigration reform, against business regulation, against the right of labor to unionize, against greater or even existing environmental protection, and on and on, rolling back the New Deal and much more.

These conservatives have moved light-years away from the moderate Republicans of the 1950s. Krugman quotes Eisenhower:

> Should any political party attempt to abolish social security, unemployment insurance and eliminate labor laws and farm programs, you would not hear of that party again in our political history. There is a tiny splinter group, of course, that believes you can do these things...Their number is negligible and they are stupid.[11]

Well, their numbers are no longer negligible! Krugman spends a good part of his book trying to account for what seems like an astounding transformation of the Republican Party. Why, in today's second Gilded Age of vast inequality and economic insecurity, could a political party be so successful with a platform that blatantly supports the rich, harms the poor and working class, and is making the middle class disappear?[12] We will return to this analysis later.

For Krugman, liberals are basically in favor of expanding all the government efforts and programs that the conservatives are attacking. For him, the US should "pursue an unabashedly liberal program of expanding the social safety net and reducing inequality – a new New Deal." Krugman points out "how cautious, how timid and well-mannered latter day liberalism has become," taking "pains to reassure the public that they have nothing against wealth, that they're not proposing class warfare."[13] To the contrary, Krugman quotes Franklin Roosevelt who "let the malefactors of great wealth have it with both barrels":

> We had to struggle with the old enemies of peace – business and financial monopoly, speculation, reckless banking, class antagonism, sectionalism, war profiteering. They had begun to consider the government of the United States as a mere appendage to their own affairs. We know now that Government by organized money is just as dangerous as Government by organized mob.[14]

FDR's rather extreme view for a liberal today gets us closer to what I mean by a progressive perspective.

Trump

This book is not a reaction to the Trump presidency. I would be writing it if the US had a liberal Democratic Party president like Barack Obama or Hillary Clinton or a conservative Republican like George Bush.[15] This book is about the clash of ideas, policies, and political directions between conservatives, liberals, and what I am calling progressives. Trump fits none of those labels. He is certainly not a conservative. That was the main point of Flake's re-making of *Conscience of a Conservative*.[16] For Flake, the election of Trump is a sure sign that the Republican Party and the American conservative movement "is lost." He sees Trump as "dysfunctional," "unpredictable," a "demagogue," perhaps even a "madman."[17] I completely agree. As I discuss later, I

6

think we will be lucky if we can survive Trump's presidency without nuclear war; even so, he will cause untold harm to the environment, civil rights, civil discourse, and the well-being of our country and its people. But I don't discuss the Trump presidency in this book, except in conclusion. This book is about the views of conservatives, liberals, and, most especially, progressives.

Progressives

"Progressive," like the terms "liberal" and "conservative," is used in various ways. I do not use it as a more palatable word for liberals, nor to refer specifically to the more "progressive" wing of the Democratic Party, although there will be many in that wing who would likely agree with much of what I believe.[18] Based on the surprising success of Senator Bernie Sanders in the 2016 presidential primaries, I believe there are many in the US who, while not calling themselves "democratic socialists" as Bernie did, are sympathetic to the views I express in this book – and there are many more around the world.[19]

More specifically, I use progressive to refer to a perspective that agrees with many liberal precepts but takes their critique of conservatives further and adds important considerations to the solutions liberals propose. Most fundamentally, liberals see the problems we face as simply wrongheaded policies. Instead, most fundamentally, progressives see most social problems as built into the very structures of our economic and social systems. For example, poverty, inequality, and environmental destruction are seen as built into the very nature of the workings of a capitalist, free market system. Gender discrimination and inequality are seen as built into pervasive patriarchal structures. Discrimination and inequality by race and ethnicity are seen as built into fundamentally racist social structures.

There are many implications of such views. Perhaps forem among them is that progressives look at our social

7

not as failures of our social systems but more as logical consequences of their successful functioning. For example, a free market, capitalist economic structure, by its very nature, despite material progress for some, yields a country, ours, and a world of widespread poverty and inequality. From this perspective, the liberal era of the 1950s and 1960s, in some ways, did offer a more socially just society than the conservative regime – the latter being what progressives often label "neoliberal"[20] – that began to dominate in the 1980s. However, contrary to liberals like Krugman, progressives, for the most part, do not look back to the US, in the 1950s, or even the 1960s, with nostalgia.[21] Those decades exhibited high levels of poverty, inequality, discrimination, and environmental destruction; they were as embedded in unfair and unequal structures as we are today – despite a somewhat more equal income distribution, advancing civil rights legislation, an anti-war movement, greater environmental awareness, and a budding women's movement. Now, don't get me wrong. All of the latter represent some progress, but extremely slow, and much of it was slowed and even countered by the policies, ambience, and the move to the right of the past 4 decades.

This book is mostly about how a progressive sees the array of social issues and problems we face (in contrast with those of conservatives and liberals). Of course, I really cannot make a claim for all progressives, since even ones who agree with the characterization above may disagree about many specifics. Nonetheless, I think my view of a progressive perspective reflects that of many.[22]

Before going further, I want to say two things. First, just a little about how progressives see what must be done. Fundamentally, progressives argue that underlying social structures must be changed. This means squarely facing and fighting patriarchy, racism, heterosexism, and ableism (that leads to discrimination against people with disabilities). Even many liberals might th these sentiments, even though they tend not to see or talk about these as underlying structures. The question I imagine bothering some readers right now is whether that also means moving beyond capitalism and, if so, to what? Whether capitalism can be tamed to operate in the social interest is an open question, as are what the alternatives might be. These questions will be examined in detail.

Second, while this book will focus some on the situation of the United States, I am equally concerned with a global view. US structures are part of a world system, and we cannot separate ourselves from what is happening internationally. Ameliorating or resolving our social problems requires that we understand the global nature of these problems. Moreover, much of my work has been international, and I draw on that experience for my progressive views and for the analysis here. Before proceeding to give you an overview of the book, I want to tell you a little bit about myself.

My Background

I was born in New York City in 1947. I was raised mostly in New York with a couple of stints in New Jersey and California. I went to Queens College, part of the City University of New York system. I was basically a liberal arts major, taking a lot of introductory courses across fields, but my official major was math. I started graduate school in 1968 at Stanford University, studying in a joint program between the Economics Department and the Business School. At Stanford, I got an MA in economics, an MBA, and a PhD that focused on economics and public policy.

The time was the late 1960s, and although the Business School (my academic home) was pretty conservative, there were many liberals and some budding progressives like me. Like many of my generation, I was against the Vietnam War. I avoided the draft by joining the Reserve Officer's Training Corps (ROTC). However, after a year-and-a-half in ROTC, I told my commanding officer I was against the war and they let me transfer into the Army

Reserves where I served for another four-and-a-half years. I am probably one of the very few people in the US who went through Army basic training twice, once with ROTC and then once again in the Reserves.

The sixties influenced me greatly, as it did a large segment of my generation. In graduate school, I began to critique the economics framework I was being taught, as well as the stance and policies of both conservatives and liberals. I wound up looking for some more concrete applications of economics and looking for financial assistance to support my studies. There were two scholarship opportunities, one in health economics and the other in a new field called the economics of education. I chose the latter and wound up working with two economists in the School of Education, Martin Carnoy and Henry Levin. They were recent graduates of establishment programs, Martin from the University of Chicago and Hank from Rutgers University, but both were also very much influenced by the sixties and were critics of the dominant economics framework. They were a strong influence and continue to do amazing work.

After graduate school, I had two job offers to choose from. One was the Environmental Protection Agency which was hiring young economists to use a cost-benefit economics framework to go after polluters. While it was tempting, I chose an academic job and went to Cornell University's Department of Education to be their first economist of education. I have, for the most part, worked in academia ever since. After 3 years at Cornell, my job was eliminated because New York City went bankrupt, the state's finances were impacted, and my job at Cornell was state-funded (Cornell is a strange and unique mix of private and public). I went back to Stanford as a visiting professor, but by then I was getting tired of the US academic rat race and was looking for an alternative. A former professor connected me to a business school job in Natal, in northeastern Brazil, where I taught public administration and policy for 2 years. After that,

I settled back to an academic life in the US, spending 19 years in the College of Education at Florida State University and as long now here at the College of Education at the University of Maryland, College Park.

While my main work has been within universities, I have been very active in consulting on a wide variety of policies and projects around the world. I have worked on projects in over 30 different countries, including in the US. Most of my consulting and research project work has been focused on the connection of education to economic and social development, at all levels of education including primary, secondary, higher, and adult education. I have also done some work in other fields like agriculture, health, rural development, and telecommunications. Much of my work has been done for international agencies like UNESCO, UNICEF, United States Agency for International Development (USAID), the World Bank, the Inter-American Development Bank, and the Asian Development Bank. I also have worked for a variety of country ministries of education and nongovernmental organizations.

I have written extensively on these subjects. This includes four books and dozens of articles and book chapters. I have presented extensively at conferences and given many lectures and courses at universities around the world. In the last few years, I have been writing a blog for Education International, the global umbrella teachers union with over 30 million members worldwide as well as op ed pieces for popular media.

A Preview of What's to Come

In what follows, I discuss various social issues and problems, generally contrasting conservative and liberal views with progressive perspectives. Over three-quarters of the book concerns education, economics, poverty, inequality, and international development, the topics I know best, having spent the past 4 decades working in these areas. But after that discussion, I deal briefly with other very important concerns, such as health care, the environment, and war and violence, areas in which I have no special expertise. I don't do this or any of this analysis and discussion out of arrogance, but, as someone with a progressive perspective, I have views on all these topics that I think are worth expressing. Many of you may disagree with my views, which is fine. As I said earlier, I think a progressive perspective is under-represented, especially in American discourse, and my hope is that I can at least contribute to a better understanding of these views and perhaps convince some of you to consider these views further.

I begin in Chapter 2 by examining some aspects of US education. I discuss many of the current conservative reforms of teaching that are being promoted: school choice, vouchers, and charter schools; the emphasis on narrow versions of accountability and testing; the control of the teaching profession through evaluation; the nature of the racial and social class achievement gap; and the question of whether more money can make a difference. I conclude with looking at the foundations that are pushing this reform package.

In Chapter 3, I turn to international education. I start by considering the ubiquitous international cross-country comparisons of student achievement tests. The rest of the chapter is on the situation in developing countries, the international efforts to improve education there, and the problems with the attempts to do so. Issues of privatization and narrow approaches to accountability and testing are raised. I conclude with looking at how the World Bank has been pushing this reform package.

Chapter 4 examines the underpinnings of the field of economics. It is the story mainstream economics tells of the efficiency and equity of a competitive, market-based capitalist system. I distinguish the two principal schools of thought about these issues, liberals who believe in the need for considerable government intervention in the economy in order to achieve efficiency and equity, and conservatives who decry government interference and argue that markets will achieve these goals without government. I conclude with the strong liberal critique of the "market fundamentalism" of conservatives and a hint of the even stronger critique of progressives that will come.

In Chapter 5, I begin by offering a quick picture of the awful extent of poverty in the US and worldwide. This is followed by a focus on the extent of the related issue of income and wealth inequality. I draw on Thomas Piketty's work, among others. I conclude with a section on how conservative and liberal economists view poverty and inequality differently and again suggest a little about a progressive view.

Chapter 6 discusses some of the various approaches that have been taken to promoting international development, especially in terms of improving the standard of living in developing countries. The previous chapter on poverty and inequality provides the stark background for this effort. I begin with the differences between the liberal era of the 1960s and 1970s and the conservative regime that was ushered in in the 1980s. A number of key interconnected issues are discussed, especially focused on the role of governments, widespread citizen participation, nongovernmental and civil society organizations, and the partnerships between various stakeholders. Issues of globalization are discussed as are the major international efforts embodied in the UN's Millennium Development Goals and their successor, the Sustainable Development Goals. I conclude with an analysis of the extent to which development has become big business.

The previous three chapters lead directly to the discussion of capitalism in Chapter 7. Central to a progressive view is that our societal problems are not easily solved, despite good intentions, even if we were to move away from the disastrous conservative policies of the past 4 decades to the more liberal ones of the 1960s and 1970s. Poverty, inequality, and discrimination are built into the very structures of our societies, and progressive change requires transforming those structures. This chapter tackles head-on the question of what is wrong with capitalism and what alternatives to capitalism are possible.

In Chapter 8, I return to the topic of education because the previous chapters have laid the groundwork for what progressive alternatives for education can be envisioned. Here I discuss the work of people like Paulo Freire who are concerned with critical pedagogy and social justice education.

Progressives are not only concerned with capitalism. As I said above, social class and economic inequalities intersect with issues of sexism, racism, heterosexism, and ableism. For progressives, these latter issues are more than individual prejudices, but are rooted in underlying and long-standing social structures. Chapter 9 looks at some of these intersections in terms of the struggles involving gender, race and ethnicity, gay, lesbian, bisexual and transgender communities, and people with disabilities. As always, differences between conservative, liberal, and progressive views are highlighted.

In Chapter 10, I look, albeit briefly, at these debates applied to three other issues of supreme importance in the world today. The approach taken to health care is front and center in US politics, and the state of health in the world is embroiled in the same controversies. Environmental degradation and destruction may be the most pressing problem we face. And problems of war and violence within and between countries are a close second.

Chapter 11 is a brief but relevant digression. It looks at my view of the very limited ability of research to resolve the many dilemmas that we face described in the previous chapters. Finally, Chapter 12 offers some concluding thoughts.

A few points before we begin. I use the terms "conservative" and "neoliberal" interchangeably. No one likes to be labeled, to be put in boxes, so please remember that terms such as these are only approximations to views. I do try to make an effort to not caricature the conservative and liberal views with which I disagree. I think it is important to understand how others think and to not create straw-person versions of their arguments. Nonetheless, dealing briefly with so many issues, I am sure some people will say I wasn't fair to their points of view. I leave it to readers to decide.

Chapter 2

Education in the US

In the 1960s and 1970s in the US, a liberal perspective was dominant in education politics and policy, as it was more generally.[23] President Lyndon Johnson's Great Society program yielded legislation that was a hallmark of this era. Race became a central issue, and the civil rights movement became very important. Earlier, in the 1950s, the Supreme Court's decision in Brown v. Board of Education ushered in decades of struggle over our schools that continues to this day. The 1965 Elementary and Secondary Education Act was landmark legislation that signaled greater involvement of the federal government in the nation's education system. Especially important was Title I of this Act, which, among other things, directed and continues to direct federal dollars to students from disadvantaged families throughout the country.

Central to this liberal era were concerns with equity. A growing women's movement, a strong civil rights movement, and a focus on poverty in America all challenged inequalities in circumstances, opportunities, and outcomes. Despite this recognition, I see this era as one of continuing the post-World War II optimism, a continuation of a belief that unfairness and bad policies can be corrected, that government can be made to work better through the ballot box and through citizen mobilization. The eventual success of protests against the Vietnam War contributed to this belief. In education, there was optimism that attention to poverty generally, providing more resources for disadvantaged students, and racial integration of schools could yield significant improvements.

Nonetheless, this optimism about education, which today is hard to find, began to be eroded during the liberal era, partly as a result of experience with slow progress. This erosion was reinforced by two widely disseminated studies. The Coleman Report in the 1960s, commissioned by the US Congress, collected and analyzed nationwide data, concluding that student achievement was primarily determined by family background, not school resources.[24] In the 1970s, this was seconded by another major study by Christopher Jencks of Harvard University and colleagues which reported the lack of impact of education on income and employment as well as on student achievement.[25] Despite significant criticisms of both studies and their conclusions, they have been used to this day to support a more tempered and pessimistic view of the potential of schooling to effect change.

That pessimism about the potential of education to alter life circumstances took hold in the conservative/neoliberal era sea change that began gathering force in the 1980s. The pessimism about education was part of a broader pessimism about the potential of any government actions or policy to bring about a better life for its citizens. Yet throughout this neoliberal era, up to today, this belief that schools are almost doomed to fail has co-existed with a somewhat contradictory call for sweeping reform of education.

A harbinger of some of what was to come was the 1983 report of the National Commission on Excellence in Education appointed by President Ronald Reagan. Its report, entitled *A Nation at Risk*, is talked about to this day. The report ushered in the attack on teachers and schools that has characterized the neoliberal era. *A Nation at Risk* argued that the US was behind other economies in the early 1980s, most notably Japan, and that the culprit was our educational system. The opening lines of the report have been widely quoted:

> Our nation is at risk. Our once unchallenged preeminence in commerce, industry, science, and technological innovation

17

is being overtaken by competitors throughout the world... If an unfriendly foreign power had attempted to impose on America the mediocre educational performance that exists today, we might well have viewed it as an act of war.[26]

As one wag said at the time, it was a repeat of Sputnik's instigation of educational reform in the 1950s to compete with the Soviet Union – but, instead, it was as if Japan had launched a Toyota into orbit and the US schools once again were blamed for falling short. Of course, if the US educational system was in any way to blame for poor economic performance, perhaps the focus should have been on the nation's business schools where short-run profits were emphasized over long-run performance.

In the remainder of this chapter, I discuss the education reform polices put forth in our neoliberal era as well as some of the criticisms of these reforms put forth by those who share a progressive perspective. I will not offer any sharp distinctions between neoliberal and liberal perspectives – as I will in subsequent chapters on economics and international development. In US education, the shift to the political right of the past almost 40 years has led to an accord in practice, in which liberals embrace many neoliberal education reforms, reforms they would have fought against in the 1960s and 1970s. I will explain this further below.

School Choice, Vouchers, and Private Schooling

Perhaps the most controversial set of neoliberal education reforms have revolved around issues of school choice, private schools, and vouchers. When I was a graduate student at Stanford University in the early 1970s, I was part of a team that was evaluating one of the early voucher experiments that was sponsored by the US government in Alum Rock School District in San Jose, California. It didn't involve private schools at all. Public schools in the district were re-organized, mostly by teachers, into mini-schools, sometimes with several different ones in the same building. Information about the philosophy and orientation of each of the mini-schools (e.g., specialization in arts, science, character formation, etc.) was disseminated widely, and parents could choose which school best fit their children. While it was very interesting, it didn't last for long.

In more recent years, vouchers have been tried as a way of offering parents the opportunity to not only send their children to a public school other than their neighborhood school, but also to private schools, including religious schools. Parents are given a voucher for a certain amount of money that can then be used for entrance to other public schools or, if they will accept the voucher, a private school. Often, parents have to "top up" the voucher amount to afford the tuition of a private school. These voucher programs – in cities like Cleveland and Milwaukee and statewide in Florida and Michigan and in Washington, DC – have been very controversial for a number of reasons.

One reason is that the US Constitution contains language calling for the separation of church and state, seen by some as prohibiting public monies going to religious schools. But court cases have overruled that prohibition, allowing voucher programs to be used in religious schools. A second reason for controversy is the whole idea of taking funds away from public schools to support private schools, especially for-profit enterprises. Critics argue that vouchers skim off some of the more able students and leave public schools in poor neighborhoods more disadvantaged than ever before. They argue that voucher programs contribute to further stratification, making school systems more unequal than ever before. Moreover, without sufficient regulation, private schools may not offer the kind of broad curriculum that is necessary for a democratic society. Critics point out that voucher programs have a shameful history. They were first used in some Southern states that tried to get around court desegregation decisions in the 1950s by closing all the public schools in a district and giving parents vouchers so they could send their children to whites-only schools.

There is a lot of debate around whether private schools are "better" than public schools. Most of the research says they are *not* better in terms of student achievement on tests. This seems counter-intuitive since many elite private schools seem to have better outcomes than your average public school. But studies have shown that once you compare schools with students with similarly advantaged backgrounds, private and public schools do equally well.[27] Moreover, private schools, even in voucher experiments, are allowed to select their students and usually don't take students with problems or disabilities.

One of the most common and growing forms of choice in US education is through charter schools. While these are publicly owned and funded, they are usually privately managed, increasingly by corporate entities. Charters are also different in that many of the regulations that apply to regular public schools are suspended for charter schools. Charters are not as controversial as vouchers, but most progressives have concerns, especially about the consequences of private or corporate control of schools and the further stratification and inequality of the school system overall. And, again, most research indicates that students in charter schools perform no better on tests than those in regular public schools.[28]

School choice, in any of the forms above, has significant problems for some liberals and most progressives. First, real choice is not usually present for most people. One limiting factor is the cost of transportation – most poor families cannot afford to provide transportation to other than their neighborhood school. Another limiting factor is lack of good information about alternatives. And even when some information is provided, poor families have less access to it and less time to study alternatives. The conservative right tries to portray choice as only fair – arguing that poor families should have choices like rich families do to send their children to better schools. But poor families are priced out of good private schools. And, since voucher plans progressively allow middle- and upper-income families to participate, vouchers turn into a subsidy for parents who would be sending their children to private schools anyway – further draining money from public schools.

Accountability, Testing, and Measurement Mania

Neoliberal education reforms in the US, under the guise of furthering accountability, have promoted an obsession with testing and measurement. This was institutionalized with President George W. Bush's signature federal education program, No Child Left Behind (NCLB). NCLB required the states to engage in massive testing of K-12 students in a few subjects, with penalties for repeatedly low-performing schools. One of the most significant penalties was the "reconstitution" of schools, by which principals and teachers were dismissed and replaced, and the school was sometimes supervised by the state instead of the local district. Studies of reconstituted schools generally showed little, if any, improvement in performance.[29]

NCLB had many problematic consequences. First, there was hardly any effort devoted to improving schools that were low-performing aside from the drastic remedy of reconstitution. As one wag put it, it was as if the remedy for a child that was ill was simply taking their temperature through testing but not providing any medicine to follow. Second, the curriculum for K-12 schools throughout the country was narrowed. Subjects that weren't tested – like history, some sciences, art, music, social studies, and physical education – had their hours of instruction cut short or eliminated. And, most problematically, after many years, there was still no improvement in test scores![30]

The successor program of the Obama administration, Race to the Top, brought little relief to the testing mania, and, among other things, promoted untried and unwarranted reforms like charter school expansion and narrow teacher evaluations (to be discussed). Teachers and students have been rebelling against this narrow equivalency of accountability with testing. Students and parents in many locales have simply refused to participate in some of the testing, and some have organized to oppose it. Teachers report that testing mania has distorted the curriculum, with considerable classroom time now being devoted to test preparation and the testing itself. Testing mania has lessened teacher control over their classroom and made teaching, for many, a much less attractive profession.[31] More recent education policy changes, like the Every Student Succeeds Act, signed by Obama in 2015, and the direction of Trump's controversial Secretary of Education, Betsy DeVos, signal further expansion of these unfortunate trends.

The Evaluation and Control of Teaching

This narrow view of accountability and testing has resulted in a de-professionalization of teaching. This has been manifest in multiple ways. One is in how to evaluate teachers. During the last decade, there has been a very successful movement by conservatives and many liberals to make the assessment of teachers' "contribution" to increasing student test scores a significant part of teacher evaluations. There are many fundamental problems with this approach. First, tests cover only a narrow range of the educational outcomes that we want teachers to foster. Evaluating teachers by narrow testing distorts education to the easily measurable. Second, students' success on tests depends on literally *dozens* of factors besides who is their current teacher – past teachers and schooling, parental support and background, resources at home, access to technology, student motivation, peer effects, student well-being on the day of the test, the school climate, the community environment, and many, many others. As I will discuss in Chapter 11, it is *impossible* for our research methods to isolate the impact of one factor – the effect of a student's teacher – from all the other factors that affect a particular test score. The statistical methods being used to isolate the impact of teachers from other factors are essentially random number generators that misclassify many good teachers as poor ones and many poor teachers as good ones.[32]

This approach to the evaluation of teacher performance is being tied to teacher pay and dismissal. Teachers around the country are being rewarded or fired based on this completely unreliable and nonsensical approach to teacher evaluation. "Pay for performance" is part of the narrowing of the approach used to govern many public activities, not just teaching, as part of what has been called New Public Management.[33] Most studies of pay for performance in teaching show no impact on raising student test scores, so it is not even an effective strategy in its own narrow terms.[34] To the contrary, the most sensible approach is to treat K-12 teaching as the profession it should be and to treat teachers as professionals. This means relying on the same sort of broad peer evaluation processes that are common for doctors, lawyers, and university professors.

Unfortunately, neoliberal reforms have emphasized the opposite. Ever since the Nation-at-Risk-era, teachers increasingly have been seen as problems. They are singled out as *the* cause of educational failures and teacher organizations have been demonized. The predominant view is that teachers need to be gotten around and/or controlled. There is a history of attempts to make the curriculum "teacher-proof," meaning that students will learn despite supposedly incompetent or unmotivated teachers. Educational technologies from radio to TV to computers have been used in this way, as are curricula in which the teacher's role is completely scripted.[35] This is the exact opposite of treating teachers as professionals. We will never have widespread educational success until teachers are given the training, freedom, and support they need to well educate our children, conditions we have moved further away from in this neoliberal era.

Standards and Common Core

There has been a lot of discussion in recent years about curriculum standards and something called Common Core. This discussion does not fall neatly into conservative-neoliberal/liberal/progressive terms – proponents and opponents come from all over the political landscape. Since the US Constitution gives primary responsibility for education to the states, curriculum issues generally reside there. Nonetheless, Sputnik, and, later, *A Nation at Risk*, were harbingers of a discourse that said our students weren't learning enough for the US to meet or surpass our political and economic competitors. In the early 1990s, this led to an effort to develop voluntary national standards across a wide range of subjects whereby the Bush Sr. administration funded groups of school and university teachers to do so. This effort collapsed as the very conservative director of the National Endowment for the Humanities, Lynn Cheney (wife to vice-president-to-be Dick Cheney), attacked a draft of the history standards as a "warped and distorted version of the American past in which it becomes a story of oppression and failure."[36] This became a very hot, very public debate about the political nature of such standards. Liberals and progressives lost this debate very decidedly; the US Senate even wound up concerning themselves with this topic and passed a resolution condemning the history standards by a vote of 99-1! The effort to develop national standards in all subjects was abandoned, and the subject "became radioactive to political leaders."[37]

But only for a while. Persistent attacks on the "dumbing down" of US schools and the decline of basic learning and knowledge – none of which was true[38] – led to renewed attention to standards. The greater attention to accountability and testing also propelled this interest. While in the 2000s, most states developed their own curriculum standards, dissatisfaction with their wide variation led state governors and state commissioners of education to start a process in 2009 to develop the Common Core State Standards (CCSS) in English and math. The Obama administration's successor to NCLB, Race to the Top, made state adoption of CCSS a requirement for receiving its federal funds. Not surprisingly, 42 states adopted these standards. Three more had adopted the standards and then opted out – as a result of a movement by conservatives who argued that CCSS was an unwarranted federal intrusion, interfering with states' rights to develop their own education. Some liberals and progressives have also been critical of CCSS, pointing out the business interests of publishers, testing companies, and consultants behind it[39] as well as its narrow vision of education conforming to producing skills for capitalist corporations.[40]

The Achievement Gap

Considerable attention has been focused on the "achievement gap" in US K-12 schooling. By this is usually meant the persistent and large gap between the test scores of white children vs. minority children or between children from well-off families vs. low-income families. NCLB legislation was explicitly promoted to help close these achievement gaps. It did nothing to close them. These gaps have long been present, but only in the last decade or two have they received the attention of education policymakers. These gaps are evident at the very beginning of school, in kindergarten or first grade, and widen at higher levels of schooling. Recent research has shown some decrease in the racial gap but it is still wide, and the income gap remains substantial.[41]

Causes and remedies for these gaps are vigorously debated. The most conservative position attributes much of the gap to differences in innate ability and in family and community cultures. Both explanations are essentially blame-the-victim responses. Low achievement is supposedly due either to faulty genetics or dysfunctional cultures. Single mothers have often been singled out for blame, and there is a significant amount of racism associated with this deficit view.

On the other hand, liberals, and many progressives, see the achievement gap primarily as a consequence of poverty and inadequate schooling. Schools for minority and poor children have fewer resources and more problems to deal with than suburban schools for middle-class families (Black or white). In the former, teachers are generally less experienced, learning resources scarcer, student disciplinary and motivational problems are greater, curricula options are fewer, and expectations are lower.

Poverty is seen by liberals, and especially progressives, as a fundamental cause of the achievement gap. Children from poor families have fewer educational resources in the home and in the community. Parents with less education and often with less time available than middle-class parents cannot provide the same sort of home educational environment and support. Often, quality preschools are unavailable or unaffordable. It is little wonder that so many children are already considerably disadvantaged when they begin school. These disadvantages can be exacerbated over time. Children from poor families live in communities where they see few educational successes. Many have little hope that education can offer the way out of dangerous communities and a way into employment and life successes. Many children drop out of school before completing high school, too many get caught up in crime and wind up in prison. For many liberals and progressives, the achievement gap is the natural and inevitable outcome of an unfair society.

Can More Money for Schools Make a Difference?

Among researchers and policymakers, there are major disagreements about the extent to which more resources for schools will improve educational outcomes.[42] Ever since the

Coleman and Jencks studies that (incorrectly) argued school resource differences had little impact on student performance, conservative researchers and policymakers have argued that more school resources are generally unnecessary and unproductive. They argue that we are spending more on schools than ever before and we see little improvement in student test scores over time as well as little reduction in the achievement gap. From their perspective, what is needed most is wiser use of existing resources.

Liberals and progressives generally argue that money can make a big difference in educational outcomes. They point out the huge inequalities in spending across US school districts that results from their excessive dependence of local property taxes. This has been the motivation behind court rulings and state policies to make spending somewhat more equal, as well as behind federal Title I funding to offer extra, compensatory resources to disadvantaged students. Some liberals and most progressives argue that these measures have not gone anywhere near far enough. The disadvantages of poverty discussed above are pervasive and debilitating, and major infusions of additional compensatory resources are needed to give disadvantaged students an equal education – through the provision of free quality preschool, highly-qualified K-12 teachers and principals, smaller class sizes, comparable learning resources, and more.

Who are the Purveyors?

Where do these conservative/neoliberal education reforms that have increasingly dominated the last 4 decades of US policy come from? The answer is unclear and complicated. Worldwide, as I discussed in Chapter 1, neoliberalism is pervasive, and there are many players who translate this worldview into education and other social policies – governments, international agencies, foundations, universities, think tanks, nongovernmental organizations, the private sector, and others. We live in a world system that increasingly sings one tune, neoliberalism. So it is difficult to separate who has the power to significantly influence policy. Moreover, neoliberal discourses have become the new common sense; they pervade the policy air we breathe and thus dominate the policy agenda worldwide. Here, for the moment, I wish to highlight the work of private foundations in the US that have been instrumental in pushing US educational policy in this direction.

Private foundations like Carnegie, Ford, and Rockefeller have long been influential in education in the US and elsewhere.[43] In recent years, in education in the US a different group of foundations seems to be actually setting policy, as what Diane Ravitch, a leading historian of education and education policy analyst, called the Billionaire Boys Club – the troika of three foundations – Broad, Gates, and Walton – developed and led a neoliberal education policy agenda.[44]

The three foundations come from very successful private enterprises: Broad from homebuilding and insurance, Gates from Microsoft, and Walton from Walmart. These venture philanthropists or philanthrocapitalists, as they are sometimes called, favored the neoliberal reforms of competition, choice, charters, incentive pay and narrow evaluations for teachers, results-based finance, intensive testing of students, etc. All three were extraordinarily influential in the Obama administration, and many people associated with these foundations received high-level policy positions, including Arne Duncan as US Secretary of Education. These three foundations also have influenced many school districts by offering a little sorely needed discretionary money to the districts' over-stretched budgets.

Broad's philosophy is that "schools should be redesigned to function like corporate enterprises" and that "neither school superintendents nor principals need be educators."[45] One analyst concluded:

Certainly, ideology – in this case, faith in the superiority of the private business model – drives [all three foundations]... But so does the blinding hubris that comes from power.[46]

These foundations are rarely challenged or criticized. Frederick Hess of the right-wing American Enterprise Institute argues that "academics, activists, and the policy community live in a world where philanthropists are royalty" leading to a "conspiracy of silence" about their faults.[47] Ravitch concludes that these and other foundations have essentially "hijacked" US education policy.[48] Of course, as I said at the outset of this chapter, these foundations are only some of the many players, albeit important ones, pushing neoliberal reform.

As discussed above, progressives, and some liberals, see the neoliberal education reforms of the past 4 decades as wrongheaded, as doing little or nothing to challenge the serious education problems the US faces. In fact, if anything, progressives believe that these reforms reinforce and exacerbate educational and social inequalities. I will discuss what solutions they put forth in Chapter 8. Right now, I want to turn to looking at the situation facing education globally, most particularly in developing countries.

Chapter 3

*

Education Internationally

Much of my professional life has been spent examining education globally, mostly in developing countries.[49] I have worked on dozens of projects in dozens of countries in Africa, Asia, and Latin America and the Caribbean. In this chapter, I offer my view of some of the major global issues in education. While I will focus on education in developing countries, I will start with a look at education in more developed countries.[50]

International Achievement Tests Comparisons

When thinking of education internationally, one of the first things that comes to mind for many people in the US and in other countries, most especially developed countries, are the now ubiquitous comparisons of international achievement tests. These have been going on for quite some time. Perhaps the test that gets most attention is PISA (Program for International Student Assessment) which tests 15-year-olds on functional skills in reading, math, and science. In 2015, Singapore came out #1 in all three subjects while the US was twenty-fourth in reading, fortieth in math, and twenty-fifth in science.

The US has generally done poorly on international testing since such comparisons began in the 1960s. Nonetheless, each time these tests come out, analysts and policymakers call for reform, declaring it a "wake-up call" or a new Sputnik-like challenge. Why the US performs poorly is the subject of much debate. Some attribute the success of Singapore and other Asian nations and territories to cultural differences or to their greater emphasis on testing throughout schooling (although since NCLB, this is less true). Tied to this is that these students seem more committed to doing well on international tests, whereas

US students are less motivated since they don't see such tests as "counting." Perhaps the strongest explanation for the US lack of success is the combination of two facts: that a much greater percentage of US children grow up poor than other developed countries and that at age 15, more of them are still in school.

Alternatively, often the explanation for different levels of success in international testing is sought in the differences in educational policies between countries. Finland, which has enjoyed considerable success in PISA over the years (although a little less so in 2015), is often looked to by educational reformers. Finland's approach to education is very different than that of the US: there are no standardized tests in Finland, and grades are not even given until fifth grade; the curriculum is broad and balanced; students do not start school until age 7 and have the equivalent of 2 years fewer total instructional hours than in the US; a cooperative learning model is used, not a competitive one; teaching is a very attractive profession, well-paid; private schools are prohibited; teachers control curriculum implementation and their own professional evaluation; and teacher unions are true educational partners.[51]

I think there is a lot to be learned from Finnish education – for the US and for other countries. But that does not mean that these features are the reason Finnish students do so well on PISA and other international tests. For one thing, Finland has a child poverty rate less than 5 percent, while in the US it is over 20 percent. One analyst in 2009 examined US PISA scores only in school districts where the child poverty rate was under 10 percent and found that, under those circumstances, the US would have ranked #1.[52] As evocative as some of these differences are, it is difficult to parse out the causes of testing differences – as I discuss more fully later. Moreover, such test scores are only one indicator of important outcomes of education, and their significance has been over-emphasized. Finally, few developing countries participate in these global tests, and it is to their situation I now turn.

The Situation in Developing Countries

The situation in developing countries varies, especially between low-income and middle-income countries – but in all developing countries the state of education is very problematic when compared with richer, developed nations. Some statistics show some dimensions of the problem. In low-income countries, even primary school is far from universal. There are some 60 million children around the world of primary school age who are not in school – either they never started or dropped out before finishing. More broadly, out of the about 1.6 billion children in the world, 260 million are not in primary or secondary school, and 400 million are functionally illiterate.[53] Almost all of them are in developing countries.

The issue is not only access to schooling. The quality of schooling is very problematic in many countries. Large class sizes – 80 to 100 students to one teacher in first grade – is not uncommon. Many teachers have little training, even textbooks are scarce, and facilities are not conducive to learning. Low quality schooling often combines with widespread poverty and material deprivation. Malnutrition is too common, stunting is widespread, limiting children's capacity to learn. Of course, developing countries are very diverse, and there are many middle-class and wealthy communities. Nonetheless, the situation facing too many families and children is dire.

International Efforts to Improve This Situation

After World War II there was increased attention focused on the need for more rapid international development. Attention to education in developing countries became the subject of international meetings and agreements as well as international financial aid. Most developing countries rapidly expanded educational access as a way of promoting economic growth, building national unity, and garnering political support. International agreements and aid were intended to accelerate this process. Starting in the 1960s, UNESCO convened a number of international meetings and agreements to promote universal primary schooling and adult literacy, often spelling out specific targets and dates. Despite such impetus, these targets and dates were never realized.

In the late 1980s, disappointment with the failure to achieve such goals led to a joint effort by UNESCO, the World Bank, UNICEF, and UNDP to promote a major effort to push things forward more rapidly. The result was the Education for All (EFA) initiative, launched by a meeting of 155 countries in Jomtien, Thailand in 1990. The EFA compact was an agreement on six far-reaching goals for all developing countries to achieve by the year 2000, dealing with early childhood, basic and adult education and training. Unfortunately, once again, rhetoric far exceeded reality and not much was accomplished over the decade.

Not to be deterred or give up, the international community doubled down on this effort in two ways. In the year 2000, there was a global EFA follow-up conference in Dakar, Senegal, which modified the goals a little and set a new target date of 2015. Also, in a separate effort, the United Nations developed the Millennium Development Goals (MDGs) – a set of eight goals for improving conditions in developing countries, also to be achieved by 2015. Two of the goals concerned education – one on universal primary education and the other on parity between the schooling of girls and boys (the MDGs and their other development goals will be discussed in a later chapter).

Unfortunately, 2015 has come and gone, with neither the new EFA goals nor the two education MDGs achieved. Not to be deterred or give up, the international community yet again doubled down on this effort in two ways. In 2015, there was another global EFA follow-up conference, this time in Incheon, Korea, which expanded the goals and set a new target date for 2030! In a separate effort, the UN initiated the Sustainable Development Goals (SDGs) as a successor to the MDGs – with even more ambitious targets, now set for 2030 (to be discussed later). One of the SDGs concerns education, and this time the UN process was coordinated with the EFA process so they both have the same single goal, with ten more-ambitious-than-ever targets.

For some, these processes would be laughable – if they weren't so sad. For the most part, neoliberals and liberals are neither laughing nor sad (well, maybe some of the latter are sad). For the most part, while acknowledging that none of the EFA goals have been achieved, liberals and neoliberals point out that progress has been made, and some would say significant progress. However, I, like many progressives, am outraged. At the most basic level, the international community has been promising universal primary education since the 1960s, and if we continue with business as usual, projections are that we will not get there by 2030 either – that would make 70 years of false promises for the most basic goal – not to mention the other much more ambitious education goals of the SDGs and the present incarnation of EFA.[54]

From a progressive perspective, despite the good intentions of many of the people involved, we have not been serious about achieving these goals. Most clearly lacking is the international financial aid that is necessary to help developing countries meet these goals. At the second global EFA meeting in Dakar, James Wolfensohn, then president of the World Bank, pledged that no country that was making an effort to achieve EFA goals would be prevented from doing so by lack of finances. This was a lie, the World Bank clearly reneged on this promise. By some estimates, an additional $30 billion a year was needed from the international community, and the World Bank's Fast Track Initiative, later called the Global Partnership for Education, was putting in less than $0.5 billion a year. Sixty times more effort was needed! And for the new EFA/SDG effort, an additional $40 billion a year is needed, 80 times more than is being put in. Billions of dollars provided by wealthier countries in aid to developing countries sounds like a lot of money – but counting all today's international aid to education from all sources comes only to $8 per child, a pittance.[55] Looked at another way, the shortfall needed to provide decent education to every child would only cost a few days' worth of global spending on the military.

From a progressive view, the glass is not half full as liberals and neoliberals see it. Most fundamentally, EFA, the MDGs, and the SDGs are what one scholar called "compensatory legitimation."[56] That is, they are there, not because they are serious efforts to redress the gross inequalities we see around the world but to compensate for these inequalities by promising to redress them without doing much to make it so, thus legitimating the unequal world in which we live, at least legitimating it in the short term. Progressives don't see this as a conspiracy to do harm, nor as completely useless. The promises of EFA, the MDGs, and the SDGs don't result merely from the efforts of the well-off to "do good" but are the result of a hard-fought global struggle in which those who are not well-off have pushed the system to recognize their plight and their rights. Much more about this struggle later.

Privatization of Education

A similar set of neoliberal reforms that I discussed regarding education in the US are being marketed worldwide. Among them, choice and competition stand out, contributing to a startling privatization of education. By privatization, I mean any reforms or policies that lessen the public control and financing of education. One area that is particularly shameful is the encouragement of government's charging parents fees for their children to attend public schools. In developing countries, public schools have often charged fees to cover incidental costs that their very low budgets could not cover. But this was often discouraged, and a number of international conventions and treaties have underlined the need for free basic education.

However, in the 1980s, the World Bank, followed by some other development agencies, started calling for developing countries to charge national tuition fees, even for primary schooling. They argued that it was both efficient and equitable to do so, given that they saw adding resources to these schools as a good investment and that parents were willing to pay. The World Bank actually required countries to charge fees as a condition of their loans. As anyone with a basic knowledge of economics – or just common sense – might expect, this turned out to be a disaster. Many parents simply stopped sending their children to school as it became even more unaffordable. A decade later, the World Bank had to reverse its school fee policies because enrollment rates had declined sharply. They even participated – albeit half-heartedly – in a global movement to abolish school fees. However, this movement has not been successful, and fees are still common in primary and, even more so, in secondary schooling.

Perhaps the major neoliberal reform of the past 4 decades has been promoting the expansion of private schooling. Globally, and most especially in developing countries, there have been marked increases in the proportion of students enrolled in private primary and secondary schools. In some countries, the majority of these students attend private schools. How and why did this happen and what are the consequences?[57]

Neoliberals and liberals tell a similar story. Too many public schools are of low quality and parents, as economists like to say, "vote with their feet" by sending some of their children to private schools. Neoliberals, and many liberals, argue that, on average, these private schools offer a higher quality education. And, they would say, given the budget constraints poor nations face, the expansion of private schooling has been a boon to the world, moving it closer to the access targets of EFA, the MDGs, and the SDGs.

Progressives, and some liberals, tell a different story. First, there is a lot of research that says – both in developed and developing countries – that private schools don't offer a higher quality education than many public schools. They often have students who score higher on tests because those students come from more advantaged backgrounds. What this expansion of private schooling around the world has done is further stratify the educational system, dividing rich and poor even more than they are divided in public schooling, yielding greater inequality.[58]

Neoliberals and liberals recognize that, until recently, private schooling catered to the more well-to-do. Over the past decade, the neoliberal answer (along with some liberals) to this growing public/private inequality has been a phenomenon known as low-fee private schools (LFPS). LFPS have sprung up around the globe. As their name implies, they charge relatively low fees, which make them affordable to some poor families. Proponents argue they fill a gap caused by too few and low-quality public schools. Opponents argue that LFPS are also often of very low quality, that they further stratify the education system since the very poor can't afford them, and that they have no public accountability.[59]

Progressives take the critique further. Let me start with a story. Some years ago, I attended a meeting about health policy at the World Bank. The World Bank presenter pointed out how, in many poor countries, poor people chose to be treated at private health clinics for a fee instead of going to free public clinics. This "voting with their feet" was touted as evidence of the success and value of privatization. To the contrary, I pointed out that this is simply evidence of the success of decades of neoliberal ideology in which public health clinics had been systematically decimated, ending up without doctors, nurses, or medicine. The same has happened in education, most especially in developing countries. Decades of neoliberal policies have often left public schools over-crowded, with poorly trained teachers, few learning materials, dilapidated facilities, and often not close by. It is no wonder that some parents opt out. However, while it is rational for disadvantaged individuals to sometimes send their children to private schools, it is poor public policy – it serves only a few, it increases inequality, it ignores the public interest, it neglects public schools, and it devalues teachers. Privatization is said to meet the growing education gap (which resulted from years of attack on the public sector), but all it does is replace an attempt to develop good public policy with the vagaries of charity or the narrow-mindedness of profit-making.

Who are the Purveyors?

Like I said in the previous chapter, neoliberal ideas have been spread by governments, think tanks, academics, aid agencies, and many others – having become the new common sense. Nonetheless, no one has been more responsible for spreading the neoliberal education reform agenda to developing countries than the World Bank. I even helped put together a book critiquing this phenomenon.[60] The Bank, as they arrogantly call themselves, began lending for education in the 1960s, becoming the single largest international aid agency funder for education by the 1980s. While the vast bulk of educational costs are borne by country governments themselves, the Bank provides countries with some of the little discretionary finance they have and so has become enormously influential.

The World Bank is a monopoly. There is no other institution like it. UNESCO used to have a more dominant role in education, but withdrawal of the US and UK contributions for a number of years forced it to play a much more minor role, and the World Bank became the true director of the EFA processes and more. While the World Bank pretends everyone – countries, bilaterals, multilaterals, civil society, and more – is in partnership with it, it is the World Bank which takes the lead on education policy. With its periodic strategy reports and a virtual juggernaut of research done internal to the World Bank or financed by it, it greatly influences the global directions for education policy, backed by conditional grant and loan money that ensures countries follow those directions.

In the 1960s and 1970s, the Bank took a more liberal view of education policy. It routinely argued that there were vast inequalities in education and that public education needed substantial additional resources which should be provided through expanded progressive taxes. Starting in the 1980s, the Bank ideology was rapidly transformed to a neoliberal perspective. While the lack of sufficient resources was occasionally mentioned as an issue, it was always with a "yes, but" – where the "but" was that the main issue was seen as inefficient use of existing resources and neoliberal remedies would make resource use more efficient.

For decades, the Bank has downplayed its role in lending money, trying to position itself as the "Knowledge Bank," the repository of best practice. This is arrogant and frightening. The Bank basically only looks at its own research and that of its adherents, basing its one-size-fits-all recommendations on ideology, not evidence. Even the idea of a central repository of "best practice" is frightening in a world where best practice is always contested. The World Bank as that repository is more frightening still.

The World Bank selects and interprets the research that fits with its ideology. In this sense, it resembles right-wing ideological think tank institutions like the Cato Institute or the Heritage Foundation in the US. However, it differs in two important ways. First, everyone realizes Cato and Heritage are partisan. The World Bank, on the other hand, makes a pretense of objectivity and inclusiveness. Second, Cato and Heritage are private institutions with limited influence. The World Bank is a public institution, financed by taxes, which gives grants, loans, and advice around the world, yielding a vast global influence.

There is no "Knowledge Bank," only an "Opinion Bank," and, worse still, an opinion bank with monopoly power. This Monopoly Opinion Bank (I cannot resist—it should be known as The MOB) may not be the only source of knowledge in education in developing countries, but it is the predominant producer and arbiter of what counts as knowledge. If there were applicable anti-trust legislation, The MOB's research enterprise would be broken up. The MOB's defense is that they try to incorporate *all* knowledge from *all* their partners, including countries, other aid agencies, NGOs, other civil society organizations, indigenous people, the poor of the world, etc. This is neither possible nor sensible nor true in a world where knowledge is contested within and among all these groups. The MOB distills and disseminates the knowledge *it* wants to promulgate.

While loan officers in the Bank are more pragmatic than the policy and research staff, internally and externally, Bank ideology pervades practice. Even some Bank staff complain of the (neoliberal) "thought police" in the Bank that force ideological conformity.[61] And, like the philanthropists in the US, Bank staff in the world of international aid agencies are royalty. They rarely have to face serious criticism or challenges. Again, I do not see the Bank as responsible for neoliberalism, but they have taken it as gospel and have become its chief purveyor in education in developing countries.

In the last two chapters, I have tried to make clear some of the dimensions of neoliberal, liberal, and progressive views of education. I will wait to look further at progressive views of education in Chapter 8 – after discussing progressive views of economics and development to which I now turn.

Chapter 4

Economics

My main field of study in graduate school was economics.[62] I started at Stanford University's Business School but soon went into a joint program with the Economics Department. I got Master's degrees in each field and did a joint PhD between the two programs, with an overall focus on public policy. Most specifically, I specialized in a relatively new field in the early 1970s, the economics of education, working with two leading economists in this field, Martin Carnoy and Henry Levin. Both had a critical, progressive perspective (and still do), which, along with the tenor of the times of the late sixties and early seventies, helped influence mine. But my education was most fundamentally in mainstream economics – called neoclassical economics, as I elaborate below. Nonetheless, even in graduate school, it was clear to me that there was something fundamentally flawed about the whole field. In the decades since, I have written extensively about these flaws and, in this chapter, explain how and why I see things that way.

To begin, connecting this chapter to the previous two, mainstream economists look at education as an investment in what they call human capital. If all human capital theory said was that education was a private individual investment, there would not be many issues with it. To an economist, a car is an investment, so is a house, an insurance policy, a marriage, and anything else that has payoff – in money or satisfaction – over time. Whether any specific type of education was a good investment would be subject to an individual's assessment of its costs and benefits, monetary or not, as with any other investment. The fundamental flaw comes about because economics is most concerned with whether a particular human capital activity is a good investment for *society as a whole*, that is, whether it is a good social investment compared to other investments, or, equivalently, to an economist, whether it is an "efficient" investment. Before elaborating on its flaws, let me briefly explain how these economists see the world.

The Neoclassical Economics Story

This takes us to the central neoclassical economics story of the supposed efficiency of a competitive, capitalist, market system that goes back to the eighteenth century and Adam Smith, with little fundamental variation to today. Codified at the end of the nineteenth century in what was called the "neoclassical synthesis," the belief that a market system is "efficient" rests on the behavior of an abstraction economists call "perfect competition." Under perfect competition, firms maximize profits, consumers maximize their happiness (which economists call "utility" to make it sound more scientific), all units are small so no one can exercise any market power, no one is affected by the decisions of others, there are no barriers to any firm starting up in any business, and knowledge is free and perfect. There are no big corporations, no patents, no unions, no entities with market power.

Under these (unreal) conditions, in this idealized world of perfect competition, it is argued that the economy will be efficient in a number of ways. All goods and services will be produced as cheaply as possible and, not only that, they will be sold to us at that price. Consumers will be "sovereign," that is, the market will be directed by the money "votes" of consumers – what economists call demand. Neoclassical economists do explicitly acknowledge that the more money you have, the more votes you have to direct the market toward producing the goods and services you want. In sum, efficiency means that the market produces an "optimal" balancing of all goods and services for society as a whole. This means not only that everything is produced and sold as cheaply as possible, but that the "right" (or efficient) amount of goods and services are produced. This state of the economy as a whole is called Pareto efficient (after an Italian economist), or just efficient, and it is defined as a state in which nothing can be done to the economy, no production improvements or reallocations, so that at least one person can be made better off without taking away something from someone else. That is, an efficient economy is one that gets you to the point where the only improvements are the more difficult equity ones of assessing the value of redistribution.

In neoclassical economics, this is the story of microeconomics, how assumptions about individual actors and their environment build up to a "beautiful" state of society as a whole. The second half of microeconomics concerns itself with the role of government in this idealized world. For neoclassical economists, the public sector has two main functions: to take action when the competitive markets of the private sector fail to be efficient and to achieve goals other than efficiency. This involves establishing the rule of law and handling international relations. It also involves correcting for specific failures of the assumptions of perfect competition, such as the presence of imperfect information; monopolies or oligopolies; externalities, by which economists mean situations where one's profit or utility maximization is affected by others, such as air pollution from cars; and public goods, by which economists mean goods or services that aren't divisible in ways that allow them to be easily sold to individuals in a competitive environment, such as roads, bridges, or national defense. In terms of needing government to attain other goals, the chief one is equity. Perfect competition, correcting for the market failures above, is said to be efficient, but if the distribution of income or wealth is thought to be unfair, government action may be required.

Two Schools of Neoclassical Thought

The framework above guides all neoclassical economists. While no economist believes perfect competition accurately describes any economy, all neoclassical economists believe this perfect competition model is useful for understanding real-world economies and for guiding policy. The question that divides them is how well the model reflects reality and what are its implications for government intervention. There are two main schools of thought that correspond to the division between liberals and conservatives or neoliberals discussed in Chapter 1.

Liberal neoclassical economists believe that "market failures" are extensive and serious. That is, they believe the real world is rife with market imperfections – deviations from the assumptions of perfect competition. Therefore, a free market economy needs considerable government intervention to correct these imperfections in such a way that the economy will be efficient. Liberals also tend to believe that inequalities are widespread, unfair, and not likely to be corrected by a free market over time. Thus achieving greater equity necessitates even more government intervention. In years past, this school of thought was exemplified by economists at MIT like Nobel Prize winner Paul Samuelson.

Conservative or neoliberal neoclassical economists, on the other hand, believe that "market failures" are neither extensive nor serious. Therefore, a free market economy needs little government intervention to be efficient. Many neoliberals today go further and argue that, even if serious market imperfections exist, government interference may not be called for because "government failure is worse than market failure." Neoliberals, while recognizing the existence of poverty and inequality, also tend to believe that its extent has been overestimated. Moreover, they argue some degree of inequality is necessary to give incentives to people to produce. Also, many believe that poverty and some inequality will be corrected over time through free market policies, especially those that encourage economic growth. Thus, government interference (note the change from "intervention") in a market system should be minimal. In years past, this school of thought was exemplified by economists at the University of Chicago like Nobel Prize winner Milton Friedman.

What's Wrong with This Picture?

As a progressive political economist (more on what that means later), there is a lot wrong with this picture. Much of what's wrong has to do with the real-world failures of a competitive capitalist economy in terms of poverty, inequality, the environment, and human fulfillment, as I will discuss in later chapters. Here, I want to focus on the internal failures of this neoclassical framework in its own terms.

The great feat of neoclassical economics has been to convince people that there is a vantage point to view society, *separable from concerns with equity and distribution*. This vantage point, defined as efficiency, supposedly allows one to see if the system, or *society as a whole*, is better off, such that decisions to produce a particular array of goods and services could be made in the interests of *everybody*, irrespective of how little one had, thus separating efficiency decisions from equity ones. However, if prices are not defined according to the *exact* dictates of perfect competition, then private profitability tells us nothing about the comparative social advantages and the consequent "efficiency" of producing, let's say, more yachts for rich people instead of more rice and beans for poor people. Similarly, to argue that the allocation of resources can be "efficient" even if half the world is starving to death is absurd, but that is exactly what neoclassical economics says.

I find this legerdemain of inventing a concept of efficiency separate from equity, based on a completely unreal, obviously untrue, abstraction, absurd on the face of it. If the absurdity of this framework is not obvious, one only has to look at what neoclassical economists call "second-best theory."[63] The "first-best" world is that of perfect competition; "second best" refers to a world with at least one "imperfection," say one monopoly in a world that was otherwise perfectly competitive. Second-best theory essentially asks: "If we don't live in the first-best world of perfect competition but have, let's say, only *one* imperfection in an otherwise perfect world, what are the results?" It turns out, reluctantly admitted by neoclassical economists – second best is their own theory, not a plot by political economists – that with just one imperfection, there are ripples so that *all* market prices become distorted, and Adam Smith's famous invisible hand is no longer a good guide to the social interest, and the system is no longer efficient – nor is there even any sense of whether it is close to efficiency. In the real world of multiple imperfections – where none of the assumptions of perfect competition hold – even if the neoclassical concept of efficiency had some meaning in theory, in practice it is an abysmal failure, a completely empty idea.

This fatal conceptual flaw is hardly discussed in the economics literature nor in economics training. In my PhD studies, one day was devoted to it in 4 years of coursework! I remember being astonished the day second-best theory was discussed, since it invalidated all that I had been taught over the previous 2 years about the efficiency of a market system. I remember asking one of my professors about these implications. He admitted we don't have perfect competition; instead he said we have "workable competition." But when I asked what exactly that was and whether there was any reason to believe that it was economically efficient, he had no answer. I believe the whole neoclassical framework is a house of cards that only stays afloat because no one studying it looks too closely until they have imbibed years of indoctrination in graduate school programs in economics.

For me, the essential problem with neoclassical economics is captured in a story that progressive political economist Martin

Carnoy tells. Milton Friedman was a professor of Martin's at the University of Chicago. When Friedman came to Stanford University 20 years later, Martin made an appointment to see him with no real agenda. Friedman, knowing of Martin's radical proclivities, started talking to him about the "seven sisters" oil companies. While this oligopoly is a clear violation of economists' notions of a competitive marketplace, Friedman proceeded to offer a detailed argument as to why they really mirrored a perfectly competitive market. Martin left there astonished, partly because of the topic Friedman chose and partly because of Friedman's analysis. In the end, Martin says, he realized that his only chance of refuting Friedman's argument was if he had stopped him at the very beginning and questioned his starting assumptions. That's the fundamental problem with neoclassical economics. If you don't challenge their initial assumptions, neoclassical economists are off to the races, spinning yarns about the fictitious idea of the overall economic efficiency for society as a whole. I think that this is how neoclassical economics turns out so many economists uncritical of the framework. They begin the first few weeks of their doctoral coursework making a set of totally unrealistic assumptions and then spend the next 4 or 5 years assuming them to construct an amazing set of false implications and conclusions. By the time they get their PhD, the assumptions are unquestioned.

The one significant benefit of a market system is that it does not need central coordination. Goods appear on the shelves of stores and services are offered without some central planner having to determine what is needed – through a decentralized response to supply and demand. This was a major failure of a command economy like the former Soviet Union that was always experiencing shortages or surpluses of goods because coordinating what is needed or desired is simply too complicated. But this does not mean that markets are virtuous in any other way and the whole idea of markets being efficient in the sense economists use the term is empty. Returning to education as an example, neoclassical economists' calculations of rates of return to different types of education are completely devoid of *social* meaning. More limited definitions of efficiency may still be useful, such as calling for fewer dropouts or improved learning, but that is quite different than a statement that primary education is a more efficient investment than higher education because it has a higher rate of return. This type of social cost-benefit calculus is completely invalid.

A Note on Macroeconomics

It used to be assumed that a highly competitive economy would have low unemployment, low inflation, and sufficient economic growth over time. In practice, this did not happen. In the 1930s, John Maynard Keynes revolutionized neoclassical economics by trying to explain why these aggregate measures of the health of an economy did not behave as was initially theorized. This was the beginning of the field of macroeconomics that analyzes how these aggregate measures behave and policies that can affect them. Contrary to the one overall agreed-upon story of microeconomics discussed above, there are numerous macroeconomic theories, although like everything else in neoclassical economics they are anchored to the fictitious microeconomics story of perfect competition and the idea of overall system efficiency. Here, I just want to say a few words about GNP.

In practice, in the real world, we would like to have some idea of the total value of what is produced, the "size of the pie," separate from its distribution. In practice, this is what gave rise to economists' idea of GNP. And, you would think, that maybe this can be a practical way of getting at efficiency in the sense that if, for example, you could use the same resources at hand, through some rearrangements, to produce a higher GNP, you could say the system is more efficient. But, unfortunately, you can't say that in the economic sense of efficiency. Producing a higher GNP means, in effect, more yachts going to some people or more rice and beans to others. Any change in this supposed efficiency measure is always a change in distribution as well, so there is no separate accounting of whether some fictitious idea of "society as a whole" is better off without somehow evaluating the value of the changing distribution of who gets what.

To confuse the matter more, GNP is an awful measure of the total value produced by an economy, as has been extensively critiqued.[64] For example, GNP doesn't count household production, the work involved in raising children and running a household, work that falls mainly to women in developed and developing countries. On the other hand, it actually counts environmental destruction as adding to GNP, so using up natural resources is positive, as is repairing earthquake damage. But the biggest problem with GNP, as a size of the pie measure, is that once you leave aside the absurdity of the neoclassical story of perfect competition, prices have no social meaning as arbiters of efficiency. Prices exist obviously, but they connote nothing of an invisible hand acting in the social interest. Prices are practical guides to the constraints firms and consumers face at any given moment, but they are arbitrary, formed by supply, demand, market power, what firms can get away with. They are socially and institutionally determined. Changing prices will change GNP. A larger GNP does not mean that "we" are better off because there is no "we," no "society as a whole" as economists like to use the term. A larger GNP simply means that a different array of goods and services is produced and distributed to different people. There is nothing more efficient about one outcome vs. another, no economically valid way to keep score apart from equity. We may find it convenient to use GNP as a yardstick but must recognize how imperfect it is[65] and that it really has nothing to do with economist notions of efficiency.

In concluding this chapter, I want to point out that liberal neoclassical economists have long recognized that conservative/ neoliberal economics dominance has been problematic. As early as 1983, Lester Thurow, a very prominent liberal economist, commented: "In economics today, 'The Theory' has become an ideology rather than a set of working hypotheses used to understand the behavior of the economy found in the real world."[66] Uncomfortable musings or outright dissent have been expressed by many other liberal neoclassical economists since then. For example, Nobel Prize-winning economist Joseph Stiglitz says: "market fundamentalist ideology...serves the interest at the top, often at the expense of the rest of society."[67] Stiglitz, Thurow, and other liberal economists were mostly reacting to the current dominance of the profession by neoliberals, as I discuss in subsequent chapters.[68] Nonetheless, liberals still generally believe that the core ideas of perfect competition and efficiency serve as a useful framework for analyzing an economy.

To the contrary, as I explained above, I find that the central theoretical framework of neoclassical economics is bankrupt, as other political economists have pointed out. Erik Reinert argues that neoclassical economics has become "mathematized ideology" – the fundamental problem is not market failure but "theory failure."[69] Edward Fullbrook argues that economics "remains locked in the same narrative dogmatism from which physics escaped a century and a half ago."[70] He elaborates:

With the [neoclassical] narrative's nearly totalitarian hold on the profession's institutions and its increasing disconnect from the real-world, the faithful's belief in its bizarre metaphysic of human reality has shown no signs of weakening. Marooned in its introversion and intoxicated by its scientism and mesmerized by its narcissism, "the queen of the social sciences" has, with increasing cost to humanity, opted for a kitsch stage-show travesty of scientific practice.[71]

I basically agree with Fullbrook and the acerbic views of noted political economist Samir Amin:

> By taking the objective of building the theory of an object that does not exist, conventional economics becomes then analogous to the scholasticism of the middle ages that was preoccupied with the gender of angels.[72]

He continues:

> That such an absurd and sterile exercise as pure economics should be an object of interest to normally intelligent individuals is something to be wondered at. If anyone had set out to prove that, in the field of social thought, a desperate effort to validate vested ideologies, prejudices, and interests would extinguish any scientific or critical state of mind, he could have done no better than to invent pure economics... Pure economics is a parascience. It compares to social science as parapsychology compares to psychology. Like any parascience, it can be used to demonstrate anything and its opposite.[73]

I will return to issues of alternative visions of economics more directly in later chapters exploring international development and capitalism. Right now, let us turn to the real world and issues of poverty and inequality.

Chapter 5

Poverty and Inequality

Poverty and inequality are two of the greatest problems the world faces.[74] In this chapter I will discuss their extent, how they are viewed, their consequences, and some proposed solutions.

The Extent of Poverty

In the United States:

- About one in six people face hunger;
- Over 40 million people live below the poverty level;
- Over 20 percent of children live in poverty;
- Over 20 percent of adults can't read or read below a 5th grade level; and
- About two-thirds of children score below proficiency levels in reading and math.[75]

These statistics just scratch the surface of the significant deprivation in one of the wealthiest nations in the world. Even many of those living above poverty levels – which in 2019 was only about $25,750 for a family of four – can face serious hardships. Because of that, federal guidelines now offer free and reduced-price school lunches to over 50 percent of public-school children! And, of course, the incidence of poverty varies considerably: while 12 percent of white children live in poverty, 31 percent of Latino children and 36 percent of African-American children do so.[76]

Worldwide the situation is bleaker. Of the 7.5 billion people on the planet:

- Over 1.3 billion live on less than $1.25/day;

- Over 3 billion live on less than \$2.50/day;
- Over 150 million children under 5 are stunted from malnutrition;
- About 800 million people face hunger;
- Over 750 million don't have access to safe water;
- Over 1.5 billion have no access to electricity; and
- Almost 800 billion adults are illiterate.[77]

The true extent of deprivation of so many people worldwide is barely captured in these appalling numbers. And this poverty is integrally tied to the extent of inequality in the US and the world.

How Unequal Are We?

From a progressive point of view, the degree of inequality of income and wealth today can only be characterized as obscene. *Forbes Magazine* annually publishes a list of the 400 richest individuals in the US. In 2010, it was calculated that their total wealth is equal to the total wealth of the bottom half of the US population. In 2015, that estimate was revised. It now seems that the richest 20 individuals in the US have as much wealth as the poorest half of the US population, that is, more than the combined wealth of 152 million people![78] The Occupy movement in the US highlighted the differences between the richest 1 percent of the population and the rest of us. But as Richard Reeves points out in his book *Dream Hoarders*, inequality issues should not focus only on the super-rich: he argues that the richest 20 percent, "the American upper middle class is leaving everyone else in the dust."[79] And, indeed, 2017 data show that the top 20 percent of earners for the first time are receiving over 50 percent of total US income.[80]

No discussion of how unequal is and has been the distribution of income and wealth in the US and other parts of the world can fail to examine the work of Thomas Piketty. His 2014 book *Capital in the 21st Century*, a 700-page economic treatise, surprisingly made the *New York Times* best-seller list and has been the subject of many news shows, seminars, articles, and op ed pieces. Debates over its substance abound as well as discussions of why it has been causing so much furor. Piketty spent many years amassing and analyzing historical data on income and wealth, mostly from France, the UK, and the US. Using tax records that go back 250 years to around the French Revolution, Piketty principally tries to understand the evolution of income and wealth inequality under capitalism.

Piketty paints a dismal picture of inequality. He argues that, for most of capitalism's history, income and wealth have become more and more concentrated in fewer hands, except for a period from the start of World War I until the mid-1970s, when this increasing divergence was reversed, at least a little. He argues that this time period was not the normal course of capitalism and that, beginning in the 1970s, income and wealth resumed their normal course of further concentration. In fact, in our current neoliberal period – which he calls the "conservative revolution" – inequality has risen to such extremes that it now mirrors the extreme inequalities he found during pre-Revolution France (the "Ancien Regime") and the pre-World War I era in Europe (the "Belle Epoque") and the US (the "Gilded Age"). In the US especially, inequality has reached "record" heights that have never been seen before "in any society at any time in the past, anywhere in the world."[81]

The global story of inequality is even more gruesome and obscene. Some years ago, it was calculated that the richest 458 billionaires on the planet owned as much wealth as the bottom half of the world's population. In 2014, this was revised to 62 billionaires, and in 2017, it was revised again – this time to the richest eight billionaires![82] I remember conferences I attended where George Psacharopoulos, an economist with the World Bank, used to give the neoliberal argument that there was no tax capacity, that is, no space for increasing taxes. These statistics belie that argument, as I told him then.

How Economists View Poverty and Inequality

Let me start by focusing on inequality and Piketty.[83] Piketty is a liberal neoclassical economist, and his work has been praised by other liberal economists (Krugman, 2014) but criticized by the right and the left. For the most part, the right, neoliberals, that is, see Piketty as exaggerating the extent of past and current inequalities. Some see him as a "soak the rich" socialist or spouting "regurgitated Marxism"[84] in extreme, unbelievably, his criticisms of the wealthiest 1 percent have been depicted as analogous to the Nazis scapegoating the Jews.[85]

On the other hand, the left, that is, progressive political economists, while appreciating Piketty's conclusions about the extent to which capitalism leads to vast inequalities, point out that they have been saying this from Marx until now. More importantly, to these political economists, Piketty understands very little about how and why capitalism yields such unequal results or what to do about them.[86]

More generally, until very recently, most neoclassical economists studiously avoided discussions of inequality, especially neoliberals.[87] Poverty is a subject they might prefer to avoid but cannot, as I discuss below. Inequality, to most neoliberals and many liberals, is seen as benign, not problematic, as a necessary incentive to ensure effort, innovation, and creativity. Not all economists agreed. In 1980, Lester Thurow, the noted liberal economist, wrote a book, *The Zero-Sum Society*, in which he reported that the ratio of CEO pay to that of the typical worker was about 25:1. He then calculated that if you just looked at this ratio for white males, it was only 7:1. While the racism and sexism of the labor market is implicit in this difference, Thurow's main point is that a ratio of 7:1 seemed to be more than sufficient to give white males incentives to get ahead and, therefore, that greater inequality than that was clearly not needed for motivation. In today's world, with that ratio now being on the order of 300:1, Thurow's reasoning contradicts those who argue such market incentives are necessary.[88]

Nonetheless, the views of Nobel Prize-winning economist Robert Lucas reflect that of many economists, especially neoliberals: "Of the tendencies that are harmful to sound economics, the most seductive, and in my opinion the most poisonous is to focus on questions of [income] distribution."[89] Many neoliberal economists still refer to the work of another Nobel Prize-winning economist, Simon Kuznets, who, in the mid-1950s, posited that as a capitalist country's economy grows, incomes initially become more unequal but eventually get more equal.[90] This, now famous, Kuznets "U-curve" was never part of the core belief of the "efficiency" of a capitalist market system. It was never particularly convincing to liberals, and even by the time I studied economics in the 1970s, it was not widely held to be true. As Piketty explicitly criticizes, Kuznets' idea was mostly a convenient Cold War belief to motivate poor countries to follow the capitalist road. As far as most liberal economists are concerned, at least until recently, the jury is still out about the degree to which capitalism will eventually reduce inequality. Perhaps the main feature that has made Piketty's work of such interest and concern to mainstream economists is that one of their own now says the jury is in, that capitalism has yielded and likely will continue to yield vast inequalities unless something drastically changes.

Poverty being a problem is less disputed by neoclassical economists, but views still differ. Neoliberals sometimes argue that low incomes, and, indeed, the range of incomes, are deserved. This follows from the theory of perfect competition which implies that the wages and salaries that people get reflect their "marginal productivity," meaning how much they add to the value of goods and services. But this brings us right back to the efficiency framework of neoclassical economics which, in the real world, is empty, as I argued in the previous chapter. Wages – that is, the price of labor – in the real world have nothing to do with how much an individual contributes to some fictitious idea of society as a whole. Even neoliberals don't push this justification for poverty level wages too strongly, recognizing the inequity of such deprivation.[91] However, neoliberals, while recognizing poverty as a problem, will often argue that its extent has been overestimated. They point out that many of the poor in the US have air-conditioning, televisions, and cars, and that the poor in developing countries have other sources of sustenance than income. Liberals, on the other hand, even if some waffle on inequality, recognize poverty as a major, if not *the* major problem facing our economic system. Progressives, of course, see both poverty and inequality as fundamental structural failings of capitalism and other systemic features like patriarchy and racism.

Not all liberals waffle on inequality, and there has been recent work that has pointed out the dangers of inequality. In an excellent book on *The Price of Inequality* in the US, Nobel Prize-winning economist Joseph Stiglitz argues:

We are, in fact, paying a high price for our growing and outsize inequality; not only slower growth and lower GDP but even more instability. And this is not to say anything about the other prices we are paying: a weakened democracy, a diminished sense of fairness and justice, and even...a questioning of our sense of identity.[92]

Inequality has gotten so extreme that even some neoliberal economists, such as those at the International Monetary Fund (IMF), are arguing that it may hamper economic growth and even contribute to recessions such as that experienced in 2008.[93] And, in the US, the Supreme Court's Citizens United decision has led many people, like Stiglitz, to comment on the corrosive influence of money in politics. Going beyond economic arguments, a book by health researchers Richard Wilkinson and Kate Pickett looks across industrialized countries, and shows that the degree of income inequality has harmful effects on a number of social outcomes like: drug and alcohol addiction, mental illness, life expectancy, infant mortality, obesity, teenage births, homicides, imprisonment rates, educational outcomes, and social mobility.[94]

As one might expect, opinions vary as to what needs to be done to remedy poverty and inequality. This is a subject I will return to in the next chapter on international development and in the conclusion but will treat briefly now. For neoliberals, it is not clear that anything specific needs to be done. Inequality is not seen as that big a problem, and poverty will hopefully diminish as countries develop. For many neoliberals, the answer to poverty (and perhaps inequality) is economic growth; the informal slogan of the World Bank and the IMF for many years has been "pro-growth is pro-poor." As economies grow, they argue that the poor have gotten richer and will do so in the future without governments having to confront the difficult politics of redistribution.

Liberals see the problems of poverty and inequality as much more severe and generally argue that government interventions are necessary to ameliorate poverty and, for some, to reduce inequalities. Policy recommendations include progressive taxation, a minimum wage, strengthening unemployment insurance and other safety net programs, greater and more equal education investment, improvements in health care provision, and pursuing full employment. Progressives would agree with many of these policies. The late Anthony Atkinson, a noted neoclassical economist who had been writing about inequality for many years, went further than many liberals and into progressive territory when he recommended policies like: promoting labor unions, a living minimum wage, a guaranteed income, a capital endowment for all adults, and even guaranteed public employment.[95] Chuck Collins, of the progressive Institute for Policy Studies, takes things even farther, recommending these policies and more, including the broader ownership of enterprises by workers, that is, workplace democracy.[96] Policies such as those recommended by Atkinson and Collins challenge the structure of capitalism as we know it, an issue I will take up in later chapters. For now, I wish to turn to a related topic – different views of international development, especially regarding developing countries.

Chapter 6

International Development

Attention to international development, to what can be done to bring about a better standard of living worldwide, began to be of significant concern after World War II. The rise of newly independent nations, a growing recognition of global interdependence, and the brewing Cold War all led to efforts to understand and do something about "development." The meaning of development, then and now, was unclear and contested, but for many it meant raising living standards through economic growth. A common view was that the historical development of the West through the Industrial Revolution could be speeded up through smart policies and international aid. The Marshall Plan that was successful in re-building war-torn Europe indicated to many the potential for development elsewhere. However, specific development policy directions and recommendations varied and changed over time, as did even the evolving terminology labeling the target countries, including: backward, undeveloped, under-developed, less developed, developing, Third World, poorer, low-income, less industrialized, and the Global South.

Recent History

The 1960s and 1970s generally saw the dominance of a liberal perspective on development. Economic growth was to be promoted by a judicious mix of public and private sector efforts. It became clear that investing in physical capital, as had been done with the Marshall Plan in Europe, was insufficient without concomitant investment in education and other forms of human capital. International trade was important, but tariffs were also needed to protect infant industries that were trying to substitute national production for imported goods. Technology transfer, technical assistance, and financial aid were all integral parts of development policy. And, in this liberal era, some attention was paid to the need for redistribution within and between countries. Progressive national income taxes were encouraged. While not implemented to any great extent, two explicitly redistributional development strategies were widely discussed. One was basic needs policies that were supposed to directly provide food, shelter, health care, and other necessities to those who needed it. Another was equity before growth policies that argued that we couldn't wait for redistribution over the long run a la Kuznets but needed to redistribute resources to the poor now and let economic growth be directed by more fairly distributed income and wealth.

Starting in the Reagan-Thatcher 1980s, through to today, the dominant views changed as neoliberal policies for development were rapidly ushered in. Around the world, this new set of policies became ethnocentrically known as the Washington Consensus. Government expenditures were to be cut drastically, including social services. Government enterprises were to be privatized, and the private sector was to be deregulated. Trade was to be liberalized, meaning the elimination of tariffs and other forms of protection. Developing a welcoming climate for foreign investments and focusing on exports were key. Taxes were to be lowered. And labor markets were to be made more "flexible," meaning weakening unions and cutting protections for workers, making them easier to fire.

The Washington Consensus was enforced throughout the developing world by the World Bank and the IMF, with support from bilateral aid agencies who jumped on the bandwagon, through the now rather infamous Structural Adjustment Programs (SAPs). As conditions of Bank and IMF loans, developing countries everywhere were required to implement SAPs – which were simply a laundry list of Washington Consensus policies. Many developed countries also followed these austerity and market fundamentalist policies. However, by the end of the 1980s, there was a backlash against SAPs, as poverty increased due to slashing social safety nets and economic growth was generally sluggish. Toward the end of the decade, two economists working at UNICEF wrote a book, *Adjustment with a Human Face*, critiquing SAPs and arguing for protecting social services when implementing these reforms.[97] While even Bank and IMF staff recognized some of these problems, many of them argued that countries would have been even worse off without the SAPs, and these programs were continued throughout the 1990s but with a little more attention to the so-called safety net.

With the widely-recognized failure of the Washington Consensus (although progressives would argue it was a success for big business, as I discuss later), there has been a search over the past 2 decades for a new approach, a post-Washington Consensus, by both liberals and neoliberals. While the search is still on, some changes are embodied, at least in theory, in something called the *Poverty Reduction Strategy (PRS)* process. The economic crisis in the late 1990s in Southeast Asia caused very serious damage to the IMF's image as the global development architect. The Bank, always competitive with the IMF, tried to rush in to fill that gap. In the accompanying melee of institutional in-fighting and larger political processes, the PRS process was born as a "new" approach to development policy.

At the 1999 meetings of the World Bank Group, it was agreed that, henceforth, before the Bank or the Fund (as the IMF is known) begin any work in a country, they must – jointly – begin with a PRS Paper (PRSP), which lays out a plan "to foster growth and reduce poverty" that will serve as a basis for all their future country work and loans. PRSPs are supposed to be "country owned," with the Bank and the Fund playing an advisory role, and they are supposed to be developed with the widespread participation of *all* stakeholders, from other donors to grassroots organizations. The World Bank's (2001) view of the PRSP framework is that it should ensure that the needs of the poor come first.

> [This will] require a true transformation of society, driven by the countries themselves...[and which]...must enjoy broad support from the true experts on poverty: the poor themselves. Armed with poverty reduction strategies, countries become masters of their own development with a clearly articulated vision for their future...Countries are in charge, but they are not alone in the fight against poverty... [T]he World Bank and IMF stand ready to provide support to governments in the development of their strategies without in any way predetermining the outcome or undermining country ownership.

In practice, unfortunately, PRSPs are nothing like this. Country ownership has long been a part of aid rhetoric, but as many liberals and all progressives realize, aid has been strongly donor-driven. The current "sector-wide approach" of getting policy agreement by all the donors in a country has placed great constraints on developing country freedom of action. The country ownership of the PRSP is belied by the fact that the Bank and the Fund have 1200 pages of guidelines for its development, necessitating hiring external consultants familiar with the process. Moreover, *real* participation by civil society organizations[98] in PRS processes has been seen as almost non-existent, and consultation has been described as rushed, superficial, and half-hearted. Worse still, the results of PRSPs looked little different than the SAPs of previous decades with similar limited attention to social sector protection and stringent loan conditions promoting neoliberal market fundamentalist policies.

Key Issues

Fostering international development is a very complex and contested topic. Underlying the history above, there are a number of important issues to raise.

East Asian Miracle

It seems every decade or so, development experts single out as a "miracle" a country that has made rapid economic growth – in the 1960s, it was the Ivory Coast, in the 1970s, it was Brazil, in the 1980s, it was Chile. The degree of success achieved in all three countries in these eras and since is problematic. In the 1990s, the miracle was the East Asian so-called "Tiger" countries – Singapore, Hong Kong, Korea, Taiwan, Thailand, and Malaysia. This particular euphoria was short-lived as the economic crisis that hit these countries in the late 1990s dampened growth and enthusiasm considerably. Some recovered, and the East Asian miracle is still touted by neoliberals as an exemplar of what the free market policies of the Washington Consensus can do. Neoliberals and some liberals also argue that the expansion and improvement of education in these countries was also responsible for their economic growth.

But were the successes of these countries really due to following free market policies and advancing education? There are a number of alternative explanations from liberals and progressives. Actually, in most of these countries, governments intervened in markets in ways neoliberals find unacceptable. Most of these countries followed what economists call "industrial policies," by which governments give incentives to the private sector to develop certain sectors of the economy. Additionally, all of these countries provided gateways to doing business with China, which was often difficult for businesses to enter directly. Lastly, most of these countries were led by strongmen or the military and were very stable, providing safe havens for foreign capital investment. Thus, some liberals and all progressives raise significant doubts about using these countries as poster children for the impact of free market policies.

What's Wrong with Government?

The role of governments in promoting and implementing policies to improve development is subject to debate. For neoliberals, governments are inherently bad. Think of Barry Goldwater, the Tea Party, and a lot of Trump rhetoric. Remember the neoliberal economist slogan, "government failure is worse than market failure." Why are governments bad? Neoliberal economists have an elaborate rationale that boils down to their belief that people who work for government are too distant from the needs of consumers of social services combined with their being basically self-interested, thus not really caring about the needs of those whom they are supposed to be serving. This is elaborated in their "principal-agent theory" which argues that, for example, in education, the principals are the parents and students but the agent is a somewhat or very distant government. For neoliberals, social services are best provided directly to consumers through the market, which is why, for example, they favor parental choice through vouchers for education.

For many liberals and most, if not all, progressives, this misses two important considerations. One is that we cannot and should not leave all decisions in the hands of individuals. We, as a society, have many decisions that must be made collectively because leaving them to individuals can result in harm. Parents, for example, may not send their children to school or choose to send them to racist or sexist schools. Neoliberals essentially want to turn what needs to be determined by democratic participation over to private control. Another consideration is that the neoliberal belief in exclusively self-interested economic actors is not a portrayal of the real world. Yes, there is self-interest, and even corruption, in governments, but there are also many civil servants and politicians who are trying to do a good job of representing and balancing the individual and collective interests of others. And remember my earlier point that self-interest in the private sector does not follow any invisible hand to yield what is good for society. Neoliberals have an extremist ideology embodied in their market fundamentalist views.

Participation

Many development scholars and practitioners have written about the need for participation by those affected by development policies. But what is meant by that participation varies considerably.[99] For neoliberals, it mostly means, as above, participation through choice in the marketplace. There is actually a standard neoclassical economics textbook whose title for me captures the essence of the neoliberal perspective: *Participation Without Politics*! Neoliberals want to take the politics out of providing social services like education and health care by privatizing them and letting people participate as consumers.

While some liberals favor some privatization of some government services, most recognize the need for governments to represent and act in accordance with collective interests. They see participation not as converting all development strategies to consumer participation in various marketplaces but as mechanisms through which those affected by development policies and programs can offer input to improve them. Liberal economists generally see participation as instrumental, as a way to consult with those affected in order to improve development outcomes.

For progressives, participation is more an end in itself. Sure, it is a way to improve development outcomes, but as or more importantly, thorough participation, not just consultation, is an essential feature of a truly democratic society. For progressives, participation goes beyond doing traditional "needs assessments" or formative evaluations of development programs. There needs to be widespread participation at every step of the process: in problem definition, in examining and choosing among policy alternatives, and in program management, implementation, and evaluation. This is all in line with progressives' calls for a more participatory democracy as I will elaborate later.

NGOs and Civil Society

Nongovernmental organizations (NGOs) and other civil society organizations (CSOs) – community-based organizations, local associations, religious and traditional organizations, trade unions, social movements – have featured prominently in discussions of development for decades. Some liberals and progressives see NGOs and other CSOs as having the potential for a "third way," referring to means and principles of societal organization other than State and market.[100]

My own experience, over many years, working in diverse contexts – such as with programs for street children in Brazil, girls' and women's education in Guatemala, social and economic development in Mozambique – underscores the progressive potential of NGOs. They often run the most interesting, innovative social programs with a commitment to grassroots participation and social justice. Along with this, as one might expect, some of the most committed social activists I have worked with have been in NGOs and other types of CSOs.

Nonetheless, there is another sense in which the NGO sector has been an integral part of a system that reinforces unequal development. The incredibly rapid expansion of NGOs after 1980 has been a consequence of the neoliberal focus on privatization and curtailing government. Following neoliberal ideology, bilateral and multilateral aid agencies wanted to avoid funding governments, so contracted with NGOs instead to provide social services. Cut-throat competition developed among NGOs for funding. Those that succeeded often took a more apolitical stance, if not openly right-wing, and followed the development agenda of their funders, or, at least, did not directly challenge it. NGOs thus have become the new temp workers of development, useful to international agencies, but easily discarded as circumstances change and consequently too often limited in their ability to promote a more progressive development agenda.

Systemically, from a progressive perspective, the expansion of NGOs has contributed to maintaining poverty and inequality by contributing to the delegitimation of the State. Most NGO projects are small scale, doing little to change widespread deprivation and marginalization. Nonetheless, the situation is contradictory. There are still many NGOs and other CSOs with a progressive outlook. There are even instances of progressive partnerships between governments and CSOs, as in Brazil where CSOs are an integral part of official child protection services. The serious commitment many CSOs still have to grassroots activism, participatory democracy, and social justice combined with unprecedented ability to network nationally and globally does open the possibility of transforming State and market in new ways, perhaps even a third way, toward a fair and sustainable development.

Partnerships

I am not able to think of a term that has so rapidly been diffused in development circles as partnership. "Partnership" has been easier to accept by neoliberals than earlier terms, like "empowerment" or "participation," which had to be coopted from their original association with progressive critical views of development theory and practice.[101] There have always been joint undertakings, of course, but nowadays most projects have multiple partners, and almost no agency undertakes a project completely alone. A principal rationale for expanding partnerships has been the clear failure of many very successful-looking development projects to be expanded to a scale where they can have a significant impact. In theory, partners working together can make this happen, through pooling resources and better coordination and management.

While the idea of partnerships may seem benign, there are problems. One of the most appealing elements of the rhetoric on partnering has been the idea of multilateral and bilateral aid agencies collaborating with NGOs and other CSOs, with the rationale of involving grassroots participation and local knowledge. However, as we saw above, such "partners" most often become contractors, simply carrying out the demands and policies of their neoliberal funders. And the rhetoric is to partner with everyone! With the PRSPs, the Bank and the Fund claim to partner with governments, parents and communities, the poor, NGOs and foundations, the private sector, unions, and international, regional, and bilateral organizations. This is partnering with a vengeance: no one is left out. But this isn't really done in practice, and what is done isn't really partnering. Partnering implies some degree of equality among the partners. In practice, all these actors have very different influence and power.

The emphasis on "sector-wide approaches" to development is supposed to get all the partners together to "help" countries determine priorities. Calls for "harmonizing" donor agency priorities make donor power even more monolithic as recipients of aid become even less able to find space to follow their own agendas. Similarly, the emphasis on "knowledge management" by the World Bank and others decreases diversity of thought and action. The idea of knowledge management rests on the belief that, in this realm, we are all partners, so it does not matter by whom and for whom knowledge is generated – we can pool our knowledge and let the best ideas win out in the supposedly free marketplace of ideas. This rhetoric of partnership again ignores differences in power.

One of the worst problems with partnerships is how it contributes to the on-going abrogation of responsibility for social change. The de-legitimization of the role of government in remedying social problems over the last 4 decades now gets carried to further heights by partnerships in which no one has to take the responsibility for continued failure. Failure becomes more easily excused by partners pointing fingers of blame at each other or more likely, most of the blame will, again, be given to governments. This then becomes a new and more virulent form of "blame the victim," as partners say, "we worked together to do all we could, but our developing government partners, which after all have the ultimate responsibility for change, failed once again."

The fervor with partnerships has also stifled critique, debate, and alternatives. Perhaps the most notable education partnership of the past 2 decades, "Education for All" (EFA), has demonstrated this problem with partnership fervor. Prior to EFA, World Bank policies were constantly and openly challenged by major aid agencies. Since the formation of the global EFA partnership, this has visibly changed. Formerly vocal critics of the Bank and its policies, like the Canadian and Scandinavian aid agencies, UNICEF, and UNDP, may still offer criticisms, but much more softly and privately. Some of these agencies still get together, innocuously calling themselves "the like-minded group," but they say little publicly. And, as I discussed above, partnership has also muted the critical voices of some NGOs and CSOs, especially since partnership often comes with funding from the aid agencies.

I do not at all mean to doubt the good intentions that almost all proponents of partnerships bring, but the rhetoric and practice of partnership has not brought us advances in development. I do believe that progressive conceptualizations and implementation of partnerships are possible. As we move further into the twenty-first century, we will need unprecedented cooperation and coordination from the local level to the global, simply to survive, let alone progress. Such change can be furthered by new partnerships, but not based on unexamined assumptions or, worse still, some idealized, warm and fuzzy, "let's get together" idea. The concept of partnership, as generally used today, misses and actually negates the dissent, struggle, and collective action that are necessary to transform fundamentally unequal, unfair, and often oppressive relations into partnerships of mutuality, reciprocality, and fairness.

Globalization

It would be a mistake to talk of development today without mentioning its intricate ties to discussions of globalization. There are many definitions and debates about globalization. Most refer to globalization as the embodiment of how interdependent and interconnected the world is becoming and what that implies for the economy, politics, culture, and society generally. Some see globalization as going back hundreds of years, and others see it as essentially a new phenomenon, changing rapidly, especially as new technologies bring us all closer together in many ways.

Many, especially neoliberals, see and treat globalization as some inexorable, technical process – like they treat other "ations" – modernization, industrialization, urbanization. To the contrary, most progressives see the form which globalization (and the other "ations" as well) takes as very much the result of policies which, in today's world, are basically neoliberal ones. Progressives talk of globalization as neoliberal globalization, which is the environment in which development takes place. A major debate from all perspectives is the extent to which globalization has weakened country governments and made global actors more powerful.

Progressives have participated in what have been called "anti-globalization" movements that have resulted in protests and challenges to the neoliberal policies and practices of international organizations such as the World Bank, the IMF, and the World

Trade Organization. Many progressives prefer to talk about the movement as an "alter-globalization" one or as promoting "globalization from below." This stems from a recognition that a more interconnected and interdependent world is here to stay, but its shape is neither technical nor inevitable.

The MDGs and SDGs

The final key development issues I wish to discuss are the Millennium Development Goals (MDGs) and the Sustainable Development Goals (SDGs). The MDGs are eight international development goals that were agreed to unanimously by the United Nations in 2000. They consisted of: eradicating extreme hunger; achieving universal primary education, promoting gender equality; reducing infant mortality; improving maternal health; combating HIV/AIDS; ensuring environmental sustainability; and developing a global partnership for development. Each of the goals had targets, a total of 21 targets in all, some quite specific, and all the targets had indicators to examine some dimensions of progress. All the goals were to be achieved by 2015. However, *none* of the goals were achieved. (Some claim that extreme poverty was cut in half, which was the target, but that is only because they continued to use outdated cutoffs in specifying extreme poverty.)

Recognizing that the MDGs were not fulfilled, the UN began a process to develop a set of successor goals, resulting in the SDGs. These were unanimously approved by the UN in 2015, apply to developed countries as well as developing countries, and are even more ambitious than the MDGs. The SDGs consist of 17 goals to be achieved by 2030 and focus on sustainable development overall, with the following specifics: no poverty; zero hunger; good health and well-being; quality education; gender equality; clean water and sanitation; affordable and clean energy; decent work and economic growth; industry, innovation, and infrastructure; reduced inequalities; sustainable cities and communities; responsible consumption and production; climate action; life below water; life on land; peace, justice, and strong institutions; and partnerships for the goals. Each of these goals also had targets, with 169 targets in total, each with a number of indicators to examine.

These goals raise a number of interesting and important development issues. First, it is rather surprising that in this era of neoliberalism we have such sweeping development goals. Neoliberals tend to want to leave development to market forces and are generally dead set against lots of government interference in markets to try to reach even such desirable goals. One explanation is that, despite the dominance of neoliberalism, other forces are at play. I have hardly mentioned the issue of human rights up to now (I will later) but since the UN's 1948 Declaration of Human Rights there have been various international treaties and covenants promoting various dimensions of human rights. Many see the MDGs and the SDGs coming out of this more liberal perspective on the need to do something about the violation of human rights associated with widespread poverty, inequality, and environmental deterioration.

Many progressives have a more critical interpretation of the contradiction between neoliberalism and the UN goals. They point out that the MDGs are far from the first in a series of international promises that have been broken. For example, universal primary education (UPE) has been set as a goal repeatedly by international meetings led by UNESCO since the 1960s and was the key provision of the 1990 Education for All international agreement to be attained by 2000. Yet it was then postponed to 2015 and now, once again, to 2030. Moreover, projections indicate that if we continue with business as usual, we won't achieve UPE until the end of the twenty-first century. From a progressive perspective, it seems that, despite good intentions, we simply are not serious about attaining these goals.

So what is happening here? As I mentioned earlier, one

progressive scholar called it "compensatory legitimation."[102] Shaky and poorly-performing economies, increasing poverty and inequality, widespread conflicts, and the equivalent of structural adjustment policies everywhere all call into question the legitimacy of the social order. To compensate for this, actors in the world system of neoliberal globalization must introduce polices, for example, MDGs and SDGs, aimed at ameliorating some problematic conditions and thus restoring legitimacy. Again, this argument does not question the good intentions of the proponents of these policies, but it does question their effects. Simply having these policies seems to be sufficient for compensatory legitimation; fulfilling them, judging by past experience, seems to be less important. This does not have to be so. We could achieve UPE and many of the SDGs in a very few years if we were willing to devote the kind of resources and attention that go into current priorities, like military expenditures.

I sometimes worry that the SDGs will turn into a welfare program for researchers. There is so much attention being devoted to developing literally thousands of indicators which will lead to countries having to spend considerable resources simply documenting SDG progress on all these indicators. This is again analogous to focusing on a thermometer for a sick person instead of curing the ailments. Will there be sufficient resources to try to actually fulfill the SDGs? Nonetheless, the SDGs also represent a gain for poor and marginalized populations. It is their struggles that have also led to these efforts and they offer a vehicle for progressive change.

The Business of Development

When I teach about international development, I, with some trepidation, usually distribute the following rather cynical poem:

The Development Set
by Ross Coggins[103]

Excuse me, friends, I must catch my jet
I'm off to join the Development Set;
My bags are packed, and I've had all my shots
I have traveller's checks and pills for the trots!

The Development Set is bright and noble
Our thoughts are deep and our vision global;
Although we move with the better classes
Our thoughts are always with the masses.

In Sheraton Hotels in scattered nations
We damn multi-national corporations;
injustice seems easy to protest
In such seething hotbeds of social rest.

We discuss malnutrition over steaks
And plan hunger talks during coffee breaks.
Whether Asian floods or African drought,
We face each issue with open mouth.

We bring in consultants whose circumlocution
Raises difficulties for every solution –
Thus guaranteeing continued good eating
By showing the need for another meeting.

The language of the Development Set
Stretches the English alphabet;
We use swell words like "epigenetic"
"Micro", "macro", and "logarithmetic"

It pleasures us to be esoteric –
It's so intellectually atmospheric!
And although establishments may be unmoved,
Our vocabularies are much improved.

When the talk gets deep and you're feeling numb,
You can keep your shame to a minimum:
To show that you, too, are intelligent

Smugly ask, "Is it really development?"
    Or say, "That's fine in practice, but don't you see:
It doesn't work out in theory!"
A few may find this incomprehensible,
But most will admire you as deep and sensible.
    Development set homes are extremely chic,
Full of carvings, curios, and draped with butik.
Eye-level photographs subtly assure
That your host is at home with the great and the poor.
    Enough of these verses – on with the mission!
Our task is as broad as the human condition!
Just pray god the biblical promise is true:
The poor ye shall always have with you.

I distribute this with some trepidation because I don't want to discourage students from working in this field. While the poem is a caricature, it does capture some valid truths about the development business – I grimace a lot each time I read it. Of course, there are a lot of well-intentioned people and organizations out there who are trying to do good and actually can help improve some people's lives. Nonetheless, there are limits to "helping" and guidelines about what to do if you join the "development set," as I will discuss later.[104]

But, for now, I want to close this chapter by examining the business of development – and it is truly big business. Returning for a moment to the SDGs, in accordance with neoliberal ideology, many, if not most, of the resources that will go toward fulfilling the SDGs will go to the private sector. Perhaps the most ubiquitous form of partnership in the neoliberal era are Public-Private Partnerships (PPPs), and these are likely to be the funnel for most of the resources that do go to fulfilling the SDGs. The biggest expense for the SDGs will be infrastructure megaprojects for pipelines, dams, water and electricity systems, and roads. It is estimated that an additional *$70 trillion* in infrastructure will be needed by 2030 – what has been called the "biggest investment boom in human history." The modus operandi according to the United Nations for these megaprojects will be PPPs. The SDGs can easily turn into a welfare program for business, where the profits will go to them and any losses will be absorbed by governments and international agencies. Moreover, these infrastructure megaprojects will likely crowd out attention to the social sectors and the environment, or even exacerbate problems in these areas.[105]

Big business is not just the future of development, it is the here and now. In an expose of the "corporate takeover of aid," journalists Matt Kennard and Claire Provost point out:[106]

CEOs of major multinationals sit on UN panels charting the course of global development; the United States Agency for International Development (USAID) is partnering with Wal-Mart and Chevron; and NGOs like Oxfam and Save the Children have joined hands with corporate behemoths like Unilever and GlaxoSmithKline.

They argue that there is a myth about:

corporate-led global development: that companies have "seen the light" and become more progressive, and therefore should be embraced as partners. While they may sing hymns about their development "impact" and "sustainable" operations, many of these same companies continue to avoid taxes and fight against regulation.

Kennard and Provost ask:

Does this 21st century corporate-led global development drive hold the answers to today's challenges or, as critics claim, is it little more than a multi-billion dollar handout to the One Percent?

Their conclusion, along with mine and that of most progressives, is the latter.

Chapter 7

Capitalism

Big business, privatization, neoliberalism, development are all embedded in our world system of capitalism.[107] As I said in Chapter 1, what distinguishes progressives from liberals and neoliberals is that progressives raise questions about world system structures like capitalism (and others, as I will discuss later). There is no question that capitalism has directed considerable human energy and creativity into the design, production, and marketing of goods and services leading to considerable material wealth for some. It has also proved much better at delivering goods and services than a command economy, as in the former Soviet Union. But at what cost? In this chapter, I wish to tackle head-on what is wrong with capitalism from a progressive perspective – and what are the alternatives to it.

What's Wrong with Capitalism?

Neoclassical economics provides the underlying ideological justification for capitalism. From that theoretical perspective, capitalist markets result in an economically efficient allocation of resources for society as a whole, with an "invisible hand" leading businesses to operate in the social interest. But as we saw in Chapter 4, this is hard to believe even in the theoretical world of perfect competition. In the real world of multiple "imperfections" from this theory, there is no "society as a whole" vantage point, the idea of overall economic efficiency is bankrupt, and there is no reason to believe that decisions in the capitalist marketplace have anything to do with the social interest. Yes, capitalism produces goods and services that people with money want, but that has nothing to do with economists' ideas of efficiency.

One of the two biggest failings of capitalism is clearly the widespread inequality and poverty and barriers to development we talked about in chapters 5 and 6. There is nothing efficient about a world where more than half the population is marginalized, with many having very insecure lives, often barely surviving. In neoclassical economic theory, capitalism can be efficient even if half the world is starving. This makes no sense. There is nothing efficient when half the world's population is underemployed or unemployed. In this sense, capitalism is one of the most inefficient economic systems ever devised, wasting so much human resources, ravaging the lives of so many people who potentially could lead very productive and fulfilling lives.

The other major failing of capitalism, as I will discuss later, is the increasingly rapid destruction of our planet's environment. Climate change is just the most deadly tip of the iceberg awaiting us – deterioration of air and water quality, extinction of species, soil depletion, threats of nuclear meltdowns, and more that I will discuss in Chapter 10. I once had the opportunity of spending a couple of days with one of the great social thinkers of our time, Gregory Bateson. I asked him what was wrong with capitalism, and he had a one-word answer: maximization. That is, capitalism depends on and fosters a belief in endless growth when a sensible ecological existence is all about balance. Capitalism squanders the planet's natural patrimony, and measures of growth like GNP treat environmental destruction as positive growth. There is a very real danger that we are moving in the direction of making the Earth uninhabitable for human beings.

In many ways, widespread poverty and inequality and massive environmental destruction are less failures of capitalism and more the logical consequences of unbridled market fundamentalism. Under neoliberalism, government is prevented from intervening to substantially ameliorate these conditions. Market fundamentalism contributes to an abrogation of social responsibility, as today, when market outcomes of horrendous income inequality, hunger, or environmental destruction are seen as natural, not anyone's fault. Responsibility and hope for remedies are placed on the private sector. But the private sector is structured to follow private interests. When I was a student at Stanford Business School, I had a professor who wrote a paper entitled, "The Social Responsibility of Business and Other Pollutants of the Air." He was very pro-business; his point was that the business of business was business, and we shouldn't want or expect them to help solve problems that should fundamentally be government's responsibility.

Many business people today actually think the opposite. That government can't solve our social problems – and that they can! Anand Giridharadas' 2018 book, *Winners Take All: The Elite Charade of Changing the World*, exposes the arrogance of many of the wealthy:

Elite networking forums like the Aspen Institute and the Clinton Global Initiative groom the rich to be self-appointed leaders of social change, taking on the problems people like them have been instrumental in creating or sustaining…The question we confront is whether moneyed elites, who already rule the roost in the economy and exert enormous influence in the corridors of political power, should be allowed to continue their conquest of social change and of the pursuit of greater equality. The only thing better than controlling money and power is to control the efforts to question the distribution of money and power. The only thing better than being a fox is being a fox asked to watch over the hens.[108]

Giridharadas exposes the paucity of "win-win-ism," the belief that these elites can solve all our social problems by doing good through doing well:

By refusing to risk its way of life, by rejecting the idea that the powerful might have to sacrifice for the common good, it clings to a set of social arrangements that allow it to monopolize progress and then give symbolic scraps to the forsaken – many of whom wouldn't need the scraps if the society were working right.[109]

Moreover, our social problems are much more complex and contested than those of business, and there is no simplistic bottom line to guide decision-making. The rigid hierarchical decision-making structures of business are nowhere to be found in the messy political environment of government. Business know-how is of very limited use, and business charity, i.e. social responsibility, is of even less use. The latter is always governed by self-interest, uncoordinated, and unlikely to achieve anything of any scale. Moreover, the hubris embodied in some of the long-run goals of the private sector are frightening. The World Economic Forum in 2010 proposed what they called a "Global Redesign Initiative." The essential idea was to turn the United Nations itself into a giant Public-Private Partnership with business being formal partners in global governance.[110] And it is being implemented! The UN recently quietly signed, without any public scrutiny, a Memo of Understanding with the World Economic Forum establishing "multistakeholder governance groups," comprised mainly of multinational corporations, as an integral part of its governance structure. This all reminds me of a prescient 1950s science fiction book, *The Space Merchants*, in which Senators and Congressional representatives came directly from business, as in the Senator from Coca-Cola. Of course, this isn't that different than what we have now in the US with corporate funding of Congress and Citizens United and the cabinet appointments of Donald Trump.

Markets are also fragile. For example, millions of small decisions can contribute to economic or environmental crises.

Depressions, recessions, economic slumps all can originate or be exacerbated by many uncoordinated individual decisions to fire workers or move investments out of a country. Progressive political economist Robert Albritton expands on this:

> Markets are often thought to be highly efficient, but in the future they will be seen as highly inefficient and costly. Markets not only fail to take account of social and environmental costs, but they also generate instability, insecurity, inequality, antisocial egotism, frenetic lifestyles, cultural impoverishment, beggar-thy-neighbor greed and oppression of difference.[111]

The line between self-interest and greed is not a sharp one. Swedish economist Lars Syll comes on strong but makes a telling point:

> A society that promotes unfettered selfishness as the one and only [I would say "a dominant"] virtue erodes the cement that keeps us together, and, in the end we are only left with people dipped in the ice cold water of egoism and greed.[112]

Businesses talk of the fortune to be made at the bottom of the pyramid – the "bottom billions" market – that is, catering to the needs of the 4 billion or so people living on less than $2000/year, often to provide basic services. What kind of world is it where we charge the poorest people in the world for basic education and health care? Answer: A capitalist world!

Capitalism also diverts attention from its own structural issues by casting the blame for development problems on individuals. For example, in education, human capital and neoliberal discourses first and foremost blame individuals for their lack of "investment" in human capital, for their not attending school, for their dropping out of school, for their not studying the "right" fields, for their lack of entrepreneurship. Educational policymakers in developing countries are likewise often blamed for their "poor" decisions, meaning decisions that run counter to neoliberal dogma, such as investing in higher education. Often policymakers in developing countries who make economic and social policy are also blamed for not following neoliberal prescriptions: labor is seen to receive too much protection, government interferes too much in the market, and business does not receive the support it needs. Education itself is also a wonderful *scapegoat* for politicians, researchers, World Bank staff, and others because education can't be expected to fix the problem for many years, so they will never be held accountable for their advice.

It is not only progressives who see fundamental problems with capitalism. Some liberals like Stiglitz offer quite progressive views. In a section of one of his books entitled "Is our market system eroding fundamental values?," he opines:

> Much of what has gone on can only be described by the words "moral deprivation." Something wrong happened to the moral compass of so many of the people working in the financial sector and elsewhere...Capitalism seems to have changed the people who were ensnared by it...[Moreover,] capitalism is failing to produce what was promised but is delivering on what was not promised – inequality, pollution, unemployment, and, *most important of all*, the degradation of values to the point where everything is acceptable and no one is accountable...The economic elite have pushed for a framework that benefits them at the expense of the rest, but it is an economic system that is neither efficient nor fair. [emphasis in the original][113]

Stiglitz seems to see capitalism as salvageable; as I said earlier, I am far from sure.[114]

Nowhere, of course, does the right see the inherent problems in the nature of capitalism nor does it even recognize the label neoliberalism. After the fall of the Soviet Union, right-wing books proclaimed the end of history, the end of ideology:[115] Margaret Thatcher's famous TINA – There is No Alternative to capitalism! We now have the one-best system, and we just have to tinker with it and wait for prosperity to sweep the globe. Well, how long are we willing to wait? While millions are suffering and dying and the rich get obscenely rich at the expense of the rest of us? In my view, there's reason to believe that even if we wait 100 years, we will still be facing the same problems because the "one-best system" is turning out to be the one worst system. It has become commonplace to recognize that capitalism has increased material production and wealth, even Marx did, but production for whom? Wealth for whom? For the billionaires who have more wealth than half the planet's population combined.

Has capitalism been useful? For whom? At what cost? Ecological insanity? Pervasive inhumanity? As the late South African activist and intellectual Neville Alexander said: "Once the commodity value of people displaces their intrinsic human worth or dignity, we are well on the way to a state of barbarism."[116] Two progressive South African scholars, Enver Motala and Salim Vally, talk of the "searing tribulations...of extreme inhumanity" – such as slavery, colonialism, Nazism, Apartheid.[117] Will capitalism be seen as another example? If things do not change radically, I think so. I think that one day the capitalist system of wage labor will be seen as evil, only one step removed from slavery.[118] The severely unequal distribution, the fact that the most difficult labor on Earth, for example, cutting sugar cane, is paid only $2-$3 a day while others get millions a day, will be seen as criminal, a labor market system for which no one takes responsibility and which is disguised by the rhetoric of freedom.

We need to be very cognizant of the forces arrayed against

progressive change. The left has long been criticized by the right as conspiracy theorists. The response of the left has been there is no need to posit a conspiracy; neoliberalism and capitalism are promoted and enforced by *structures* that operate at the world system level.[119] This is quite true, and I don't see these structures as the result of some secret cabal. Nevertheless, while reference to the "ruling class" may be anachronistic, many of today's global business and political elite know each other well and meet regularly through organizations like the World Economic Forum and the Trilateral Commission. How many have even heard of the latter? In it are the most influential politicians and industrialists in the world, and it has been meeting in secret for decades. Neoliberal capitalist policies are promoted and even coordinated by an elite class of like-minded individuals who think that governments are overvalued and business solutions undervalued and act in concert. We must not underestimate our opponents. As Warren Buffet has said: "It's class warfare" and "My class is winning." I don't think of all this as a conspiracy to do harm. I believe that most of these people are well-intentioned. They are simply wrong, believing in a neoliberal economics that makes them better off but leaves the majority of humanity in dire straits.

Can capitalism be improved, be fair and just? I am not clairvoyant, I can't see the future. I have some progressive colleagues who believe that capitalism can be tamed in the broader social interest, like, some would say, in some places, it began to be tamed in the 1960s and 1970s. I wish it were so, but I don't think so. The greed, inequality, and environmental destruction promoted by capitalism, the racism and sexism that capitalism takes advantage of, are all extraordinarily resistant to change. Governments today, captured by elites and by the unequal logic inherent in our world system, can only with great difficulty offer significant challenges. So taming and humanizing capitalism, in my view, is not likely. Therefore, I see transforming capitalism as the name of the game. While this will not be easy, I see very real possibilities.

Alternatives to Capitalism
In 1933, John Maynard Keynes wrote:

> [Capitalism] is not a success. It is not intelligent, it is not beautiful, it is not just, it is not virtuous – and it doesn't deliver the goods. In short, we dislike it, and we are beginning to despise it. But when we wonder what to put in its place, we are extremely perplexed.[120]

This pessimism about viable alternatives to capitalism continues to today. However, for about the past 20 years, I have been fortunate enough to teach a course I call "Alternative Education, Alternative Development." When I began teaching the course, I had to search for good exemplars of alternative thinking and practice; nowadays, there are a plethora. Contrary to TINA, activist and policy strategist David Bollier proposes that the "more accurate acronym for our time is TAPAS – 'There are plenty of alternatives.'"[121] I agree. In fact, there is such a large and recent literature on alternatives, that in this section on capitalism, I can only try to give a sense of some of what is out there. (I will include more references than usual for your further reading pleasure.) This is not to say that there are clear system-wide alternatives to capitalism. As most of these authors point out, there are no blueprints. What there are are many small-scale exemplars and intriguing visions of what larger scale alternatives might look like.

Socialism is the principal label associated with an alternative to capitalism. Marx had hardly anything to say about socialism or communism, and the USSR and China are seen by very few on the left as progressive or sensible alternatives. Socialism in Europe or the Global South perhaps more so, but, of course, all of these countries are embedded in a capitalist world system, and most can be seen as capitalist but with a stronger interventionist government that tempers inequalities and sometimes provides greater voice for disadvantaged groups. Most of those who write about socialism as an alternative to capitalism today recognize that there are many versions of socialism. For example, sociologist Erik Olin Wright discusses seven: "statist socialism, social democratic economic regulation, associational democracy, social capitalism, social economy, cooperative market economy, and participatory socialism."[122] Psychiatrist and social activist Joel Kovel argues that concern with severe environmental threats makes developing an "ecosocialism" the only way to a desirable future.[123]

While different socialisms can be described differently, many would agree with Wright that an essential part of a progressive definition emphasizes "democratic power over the allocation and use of productive resources."[124] Many would also emphasize that widespread, democratic participation is a necessary feature. Perhaps the most detailed vision of a socialism that does not rely on capitalist market mechanisms has been developed over many years by two political economists, Michael Albert and Robin Hahnel.[125] They call their system "parecon," short for a "participatory economy" or "participatory economics." In it, the economy allocates work and goods through multilevel workers councils and consumer councils. Most writers do not go quite this far and still rely on a market system to allocate goods and services and employment opportunities. The hallmark of most of these visions, though, is a major change in capitalist and corporate organization in the form of moving from a hierarchical, authoritarian structure to a much more democratic workplace and more participatory politics.[126]

Somewhat in contrast to these visions for a new type of socialism is the work of historian and political economist Gar Alperovitz and colleagues who, mostly with reference to the United States, see a slow but growing transformation of capitalism happening right now.[127] Alperovitz doesn't disagree with some of the visions of people like Albert but thinks that practically it is more immediately useful to build on what we have:

> I've called the model for what this might plausibly look like in practice "the pluralist commonwealth": commonwealth because it seeks transitionally to restructure political reality by democratizing the ownership of wealth, pluralist because it embraces a variety of institutional approaches toward that end...[T]he model is designed to make maximal use of actual on-the-ground forms of democratized ownership – the millions of employee-owners, the thousands of community development corporations and cooperatives that already exist in the US serve as a key starting point.[128]

Many authors pay a lot of attention to smaller scale alternatives that are cropping up around the world as both harbingers of what may come and as indicators of what might be further developed. The "participatory budgeting" initiatives that started in Brazil, but have spread to other countries, are often discussed.[129] Participatory budgeting has been done in small communities as well as very large cities (e.g., São Paulo and Chicago) where hundreds of thousands of citizens have been involved. Through a series of meetings, it allows citizens to determine the allocation of some portion of municipal budgets. Other innovative alternatives or ideas that have been heralded include: the very large Mondragon worker-owned cooperative in Spain; "Ithaca Hours" and other forms of local currency or non-monetary exchange systems; basic income guarantees; producing Wikipedia; self-help community organizations; and the Quebec social economy for childcare and eldercare.[130] Solidarity economics examines connected cooperative organizations that have sprung up in many places, and a growing literature exists on small and extended communities' efforts to regulate the "Commons."[131]

Another oft-discussed alternative to capitalist organization comes out of the Zapatista movement. What started as an armed insurrection in opposition to NAFTA specifically, and neoliberal capitalism more broadly, has turned into a large-scale rural, communal, indigenous, participatory alternative development system.[132] Similarly, the landless movement in Brazil offers an alternative, very participatory approach to rural development.[133] Thoughtful attention has also been focused on the need to look to the development of the left in the Global South and to alternative epistemologies there that can be a basis for progressive change.[134]

Latin America has been looked to for half-a-dozen or more relatively recent elections of leftist presidents. Some are discouraged that these countries have not been able to do more to forge an alternative path and that some are turning back to center or right politics. But that is not surprising given these countries are embedded in a hostile capitalist world. The hostility and aggression faced by Cuba in the 1960s, Chile in the 1970s, Nicaragua in the 1980s, and Venezuela under Chavez show that the struggle for alternatives will be very difficult. But around the world, electoral politics are yielding some changes, even in the West: Podemos in Spain, Syriza in Greece, and Bernie Saunders in the US. It is astounding that some polls in the US showed that if Trump and Saunders had been the two nominees for president in 2016, perhaps over half of the US voting population would actually have favored a self-declared democratic socialist!

One of the most interesting and rather large-scale efforts to promote alternative development is the World Social Forum (WSF). The WSF was initiated in 2001 as a counterpoint to the World Economic Forum held in Davos each year. The WSF brings together tens of thousands of activists from around the globe who meet to share and explore alternatives related to education, housing, the environment, health, transportation, food, and capitalism more generally. Participants return home and network with millions more. Sociologist Boaventura de Sousa Santos calls the WSF the "most consistent manifestation of counterhegemonic globalization."[135] He goes on to say that noted activist Walden Bello was right to argue that WSF organizers and participants had:

> the realization they needed one another in the struggle against global capitalism and that the strength of the fledgling global movement lay in a strategy of decentralized networking that rested not on the doctrinal belief that one class was destined to lead the struggle but on the reality of common marginalization of practically all subordinate classes, strata, and groups under the reign of global capital.[136]

None of these writers who describe practical alternatives and possible visions of alternatives to capitalism are deterministic, dogmatic, or doctrinaire, as the left is often caricatured. As I said earlier, they offer no blueprints or grand designs, which, as Noam Chomsky says, would be an "act of hubris...usurp[ing] the rightful role of future citizens in determining their own lives and relations."[137] The future will and needs to be determined by struggle and by democratic deliberation. Most of these authors see the many social movements around the world as a principal mechanism for progress, for actually developing and implementing alternatives to capitalism, movements such as: the anti/alter-globalization movement, the women's movement around the world, the climate justice movement, the landless movement in Brazil, the Dalit movement in India, labor movements, the Arab Spring, Occupy around the globe, the Indignados in Spain, anti-austerity in Europe, the civil rights movement in the US, and many others.

To conclude this chapter, let me return to the point I made

earlier that not all progressives believe that capitalism is beyond salvage. There is a point at which progressive views shade into more liberal views of the economy and society. Liberal economists like Jeffrey Sachs, Joseph Stiglitz, and Paul Krugman are very critical of neoliberal capitalism. Robert Reich's recent book, *Saving Capitalism*, offers a litany of liberal reforms to curb inequality, poverty, and environmental destruction. George Lakey's book, *Viking Economics*, similarly offers a list of progressive reforms that Nordic countries have enacted.[138] However, I still think, along with the many authors referenced in this chapter, that more is needed and more is possible, even if there are no blueprints.

And there are many who agree. As above, a lot of people are thinking about and working on larger scale alternatives. As examples, look at the work of Michael Albert and Robin Hahnel on participatory economics – google Parecon. Or the organization started by Gar Alperovitz and Gus Speth – google the amazing Next System Project. Or the new initiative started by Yanis Varoufakis and Jane (wife of Bernie) Sanders to bring all of us together – google Progressive International. Or the work of Gustavo Esteva – on what he and others are calling Crianza Mutua – Mutual Upbringing – in which representatives of the Zapatista community have been meeting with other alternative communities around the world to flesh out principles and approaches to living very differently on this planet in what some call a radical pluralism – google the wonderful Global Tapestry of Alternatives.

Most of my students were born into a world of neoliberal capitalism and have never even seen the more liberal era of the 1960s and 1970s (at least in some countries). But I tell them that history is long and structures change. Capitalism is a recent development in human history. I like the quote from Ursula LeGuin: "We live in capitalism. Its power seems inescapable. So did the divine right of kings."[139] It is hubris to think that we are at the end of history, that we have found the one-best system. And the multiple crises and fundamental problems that come with capitalism may move us toward alternatives sooner than we think!

Chapter 8

Implications for Education

In chapters 2 and 3, I discussed neoliberal and liberal views of education and offered some progressive critiques.[140] For capitalism to change, education must change. Progressives see the dominant neoliberal focus on competition and choice, privatization, testing and measurement, very limited investment, and very narrow views of efficiency as wrongheaded. Fully-resourced public education that educates the whole person is essential. Moreover, given their critique of the capitalist context of education, progressives see a need for fundamental changes in the approach to and content of schooling. Andre Gorz wrote of non-reformist reforms, that is, reforms that challenged underlying oppressive structures like capitalism, not simply offering superficial reformist changes.[141] But what constitutes a non-reformist education reform from a progressive view? One can never be sure, as capitalism and other world system structures are very resilient and coopt many reforms – so what turns out to be a real alternative will best be seen over the longer haul. That being said, the principal alternatives to capitalist education come from the many efforts to elucidate the theory and practice of critical pedagogy.

Critical pedagogy has its origins in the extraordinary work of Paulo Freire, although many earlier alternatives that challenge capitalism and other oppressive structures can be found.[142] While definitions and characteristics are debated, sometimes vigorously, progressive educators Michael Apple, Wayne Au, and Luis Gandin open their exposition with:

Critical pedagogy...broadly seeks to expose how relations of power and inequality (social, cultural, economic) in their myriad forms, combinations, and complexities, are manifest and challenged in the formal and informal education of children and adults...In addition, a more robust understanding of critical pedagogy...is based increasingly in a realization of the importance of the multiple dynamics underpinning the relations of exploitation and domination in our societies. Issues surrounding the politics of redistribution (exploitative economic processes and dynamics) and the politics of recognition (cultural struggles against domination in our societies and struggles over identity), hence, need to be jointly considered.[143]

I do not have the space to delve into the many debates about the theory and praxis of critical pedagogy but will highlight a few points. For most advocates, critical pedagogy is not a pedagogical method, but a broad, evolving framework.[144] One salient disagreement is about how much attention to focus on what happens within the classroom:

Taking a narrow view on Freire's theory might...lead one to believe that the ability to engage in progressive "educational projects" is the best we can hope for – the idea that the most we can do is effect change in our own classrooms and empower students, one at a time, primarily in terms of how we teach them.[145]

These authors reject that view and argue critical pedagogy demands that teachers and students engage outside the classroom in pursuit of progressive societal changes. Progressive educator Peter McLaren offers some agreement for attention beyond the classroom:

[C]ontemporary critical pedagogy needs to rescue Freire's work from the reformists who wish to limit his legacy to its contribution to consciousness-raising [in the classroom].[146]

The central issue here is the extent to which teachers and students engaging in critical pedagogy confine their activities to the classroom vs. the extent to which they engage in the broader struggles against capitalism and other oppressive structures in their community, as well as the nation and the world.

Regardless of the position taken on this debate, what happens within the classroom and school system is, of course, a central part of critical pedagogy. Moreover, critical pedagogy comes in many forms, often without the critical pedagogy label but explicitly or implicitly drawing on its concepts. For example, there is a lot of attention focused on social justice education. Bree Picower argues that social justice education:

> necessitates the ability for educators to engage on three levels. The first is for teachers to have a recognition and political analysis of injustice and how it operates to create and maintain oppression on multiple levels. The second is teachers' willingness and ability to integrate this analysis into academic teaching in the classrooms. The third is that teachers must have the mindsets and the skills to expand their social justice work outside the classroom as activists, with students and on their own, to combat multiple forms of oppression.[147]

Social justice education and critical pedagogy are therefore intimately related. So are other forms of critical education alternatives. For example, while some efforts at multicultural education are superficial, there is a large literature on more critical approaches to multicultural education that explicitly draw upon critical pedagogy.[148] While there has been a long liberal literature on democracy and education,[149] some work on democratic schools fits very well with a critical pedagogy.[150]

There are also efforts that combine ecological education and critical pedagogy.[151] Similarly, while there are liberal visions of citizenship education, there are also ones that have a much more critical pedagogy slant.[152] There are also other literatures and practices that tie closely to the approach of critical pedagogy such as "anti-oppressive, anti-racist education as well as queer, woman, and disability studies [and] critical race theory."[153]

Freire has been extremely influential. Educational alternatives abound in practice. It is likely that hundreds of thousands or perhaps even millions of teachers around the globe engage in forms of critical pedagogy. Sometimes, whole school systems do. Freire himself was Secretary of Education for the city of São Paulo.[154] Brazil has other significant examples. The Citizen School movement has built a sizable democratic, participatory, Freirean-based education system.[155] In Brazil also, there are the Landless Movement schools, founded by some of the poorest people in all the world, often living off agricultural labor, now organized and politically influential, with a large system of very participatory, democratic, Freirean-based schools.[156] These schools teach – and exemplify by their very structure – the role of education in preparing people for a much more participatory and democratic economy and society.[157]

Even critical pedagogy confined to the classroom can be a non-reformist reform. Peter McLaren argues:

Revolutionary classrooms are prefigurative of socialism in the sense that they are connected to social relations that we want to create as revolutionary socialists. The organization of classrooms generally tries to mirror what students and teachers would collectively like to see in the world outside of schools – respect for everyone's ideas, tolerance of differences, a commitment to creativity and social and educational justice, the importance of working collectively, a willingness and desire to work hard for the betterment of humanity, and a commitment to antiracist, antisexist, and antihomophobic practices.[158]

I don't want to romanticize any of this. A study by Jorge Baxter of education and development strategies in Ecuador suggests how difficult progressive change can be.[159] Rafael Correa was elected President of Ecuador in 2006 on a very explicit left, democratic socialist, progressive platform. He entered the presidency with very strong backing (57 percent of the vote) and offered a widely supported platform that explicitly criticized the neoliberal, capitalist, and ineffective, almost anarchic government of his predecessors. In his first few years, he presided over writing a new Constitution with widespread societal participation, yielding one of the most progressive Constitutions in the world.

In education, Correa restructured a completely dysfunctional Ministry of Education, enacted a major curriculum reform, set up mechanisms for teacher career advancement and teacher evaluation, tripled teacher salaries, and increased resources for education from 2.5 percent of GDP to over 5 percent. Significant gains were made in student learning. Yet, despite initial support, Correa is now facing widespread criticism from the left for:

a state-centric and technocratic approach to reform...[an] over-centralized model of school management...a reductionist approach to quality...[and] diminishing spaces for debate, deliberation and participation around the reform.[160]

Correa is even often accused of following a neoliberal approach. While this is a very complex story, Baxter's very interesting analysis suggests that while Correa might have been sensible in starting with a state-centric approach given the dysfunctional neoliberal government he inherited, he needed to, after a time, switch gears to the sort of participatory governance guaranteed by the new Ecuadoran Constitution.

There is a history of left governments turning autocratic – Russia, China, Cuba are clear examples, but also countries like Nicaragua and Venezuela. Some part of this can be blamed on the hostility and aggression these countries faced from most of the international community, but part may be due to the corrupting influence of attaining power. There have, of course, been many left governments that have not succumbed to this, although generally these are Western countries where democracy has longer roots. But there are also exemplars, despite problems, from Latin America – Brazil, Chile, Uruguay, and others.

So progressive change will be difficult. But what choice is there? Capitalism has been so terrible for so long for so many – as are other oppressive structures of our world system as discussed below.

Chapter 9

Intersections

As intimated at a number of points above, progressives do not see capitalism as the only or necessarily the most important oppressive structure that the world faces today. Progressives working on issues of sexism, racism, heterosexism, disability, and others see the problems posed in these areas as more than individual prejudices but as rooted in underlying and long-standing social structures. The intersection of capitalism and other oppressive structures is key to understanding marginalization in today's world and in challenging it. In academia, I see a remarkable confluence of critical perspectives. While they cross disciplines and applied fields, these alternative theories, such as the following, are very much interrelated: dependency, world systems, critical, progressive economic, economic reproduction, cultural reproduction, resistance, feminist standpoint, gender and development, socialist feminist, critical race, queer, intersection, critical postmodern, post-structural, post-colonial, and critical pedagogy. And this does not include all the related critical theories within each social science and applied field.

I am not saying that these theories offer identical perspectives,[161] just that they share essential commonalities with respect to addressing the two major questions social theories face: "How do we understand our social world?" and "What can we do about it?" In terms of understanding, most fundamentally, all these theories are focused on marginalization. They see the world as composed of systems and structures that maintain, reproduce, and legitimize existing inequalities. From these perspectives, inequalities are not system failures, but the logical consequence of successful system functioning. In terms of what to do, while most of these theories recognize that reproduction of disadvantage, inequality, and discrimination is pervasive, they also agree that there are serious challenges to reproduction. There is general agreement that those challenges have two interrelated sources. One is that the systems and structures that dominate are not monolithic but have cracks and spaces that are pervaded by contradictions, such as that between the stated value of political democracy and the reality of economic authoritarianism or that between the stated value of human equality and the reality of systematic discrimination. The other challenge comes from a belief in human agency, meaning that oppression can be recognized and fought individually and collectively.

Understanding a progressive perspective in today's world requires an understanding of how progressives view forms of marginalization, other than economic. In this chapter, I discuss gender, race and ethnicity, sexual orientation, and disability.

Gender

I became a feminist – or perhaps I realized that I was one – when I read Simone de Beauvoir's book, *The Second Sex*, in the late 1960s. It was the time of a growing women's movement in the US, a time of "consciousness-raising" groups for many women and some men, and, in the early 1970s, the initiation of the Equal Rights Amendment. In this section, I focus on a progressive view of gender issues. I use the word "gender" instead of "sex" since sex refers to biological differences between men and women while gender refers to broader cultural and social constructions of these differences. Gender issues can include those of sexual orientation and gender identity, but I leave those issues to the section below on sexual orientation.

My tripartite division between neoliberals, liberals, and progressives is useful here, but the neoliberal label is probably not the best one to use. The term neoliberal applies mostly to economic and political perspectives. For the right-of-center perspective in this chapter, I will use the term "conservative."[162] This works well for the US, but is less used in other settings. Still, what I call a conservative perspective is seen in many other countries.

Conservatives generally see feminism and the women's movement as problematic. Many conservatives see the social and cultural differences between women and men as natural and rooted in biological differences. They often see feminism as complaining, about blaming men, and trying to gain privileges by a bunch of "angry, spoiled, selfish" women. Many see abortion as murder and want to outlaw it completely. I doubt that many conservatives in the US want to roll back the clock to when women were not allowed to vote and were treated as property, but they do not generally consider today's society as sexist. Conservatives were able to defeat the Equal Rights Amendment, arguing it was unnecessary and would have harmful consequences, such as leading to single-sex restrooms and women being drafted into combat positions in the military.

Middle-class liberals, on the other hand, promoted the women's movement in the US in the 1960s and 1970s. Liberal feminists believed that women were discriminated against at home, in the workplace, and in laws and government. Women formed consciousness-raising groups to foster individual liberation and engaged in public advocacy through protests and such institutions as the National Organization for Women and *Ms. Magazine*. Liberal feminists organized to support the Equal Rights Amendment and were almost successful in changing the US Constitution. They helped change many laws in the US that had discriminated against women and helped change workplace cultures.

For me, two things distinguish progressive views of feminism from liberal views. One is a focus on structure. For progressives, discrimination is not simply about prejudice and individual attitudes but about the underlying global structures of patriarchy. The US is a patriarchal society in a patriarchal world. Thousands of years of patriarchy have shaped all social institutions in ways that disadvantage women. The second distinguishing feature is that progressive views of feminism see the intersection of patriarchy with other structures – like capitalism. Progressive perspectives on feminism are complex and nuanced. The term progressive feminism is rarely used. Instead, progressive perspectives are considered in a host of different approaches to feminism, some of which I will briefly consider below.

In the 1970s, in the US, it was useful to distinguish between three versions of what I would call progressive perspectives on feminism. All three looked at some of the intersections between patriarchy and capitalism but saw them differently. Simplistically speaking, Marxist feminists saw class as the primary category for understanding the world. Radical feminists, on the other hand, while also paying attention to the intersection of class and gender, saw gender as primary. Socialist feminists saw neither class nor gender as primary, arguing that understanding their complex intersection was necessary. While these distinctions are not prominent today, these debates do continue.[163]

Other debates are relevant. I single out two. Black feminism developed in the US as early as the 1960s and has become stronger over time. Black feminism grew out of the lived experience of Black women and as reactions to both the sexism in the civil rights movement and the "whiteness" of liberal feminism and some progressive approaches to feminism as well. Black feminism is alive and well today and, in its most progressive form, analyzes the intersection between sexism, racism, class oppression, and issues of gender identity.[164]

Third World feminism grew out of the lived experiences of women in developing countries and out of reaction to the views of white, Western-liberal feminism. The four UN Conferences on Women that were held from the mid-1970s to the mid-1990s provided a meeting ground for confrontation of views and discussions. Third World feminism, also sometimes known as post-colonial feminism, usually has a very progressive view of intersecting world system structures featuring the interplay of patriarchy, (neo)colonialism, racism, and capitalism. Attention is often paid to what feminism means in indigenous cultures.[165]

There are a number of issues that these progressive views of feminism raise. Clearly, there are many feminisms. Each of the perspectives above have debates within them. For example, Third World feminism may be viewed differently in different historical and cultural contexts. Within and across all these progressive views, people are struggling with what feminism means in theory and practice. One locus for these struggles is the implications for the individual and society of multiple oppressive intersections. How do patriarchal, capitalist, and racist structures play out systemically and in terms of the multiple disadvantages and identities at the individual level? Feminist scholars and activists try to answer these questions.

One important issue for progressives is whether there really is a women's movement or are the fractures too deep to work together in common cause? There is no clear answer to this question, but I would say "sometimes, for some things." A telling example was the Women's March on January 21, 2017, which mobilized around 4 million people in cities across the US and more around the world. The common cause was the Trump presidency, although many more issues were represented. I was fortunate enough to attend the Washington, DC march, and the energy was palpable. It brought together progressive, liberal, and conservative feminists (although the organizers said anti-abortion views were not welcome). There were white men and men and women of color present, although not that many. The march was mostly white women. A sign held by a man of color that appeared on social media captured some of the dissent: "I'll see you Nice White Ladies at the Next #BlackLivesMatter March,

Right?" I will talk more about the potential for alliances across social movements at a later point.

Before moving on, I want to return to the issue of education to illustrate what a progressive perspective can mean regarding gender issues. Girls' education is a topic that has been on the international agenda for at least 3 decades, and for good reason. In many developing countries, families send their boys to school more than girls, starting in primary school, and, once in schools, girls are often treated quite differently than boys. There have been efforts, which have met with some success, to increase girls' enrollment rates, but in many countries they still lag behind. In 1997, I was part of a team to evaluate USAID policies to promote girls' education in Guatemala. In keeping with the neoliberal era, a lot of emphasis was placed on partnering with the private sector. Contradictions abounded. I remember a beer company foundation putting up billboards promoting girls' education, yet the beer company had many more billboards with a woman in a bikini lying on a giant beer bottle promoting their beer. At the same time in Guatemala, there was a growing women's movement, yet there was no attempt to partner with them. This was true in many other countries as well. The idea was – and still is – to treat the issue of girls' education as apolitical and not to get involved in the messier, more complex issues of the discrimination women face at home, in the workplace, and in law and government. However, from a progressive perspective there is nothing apolitical about the education of girls, and redressing fundamental inequalities in the school system and elsewhere requires attention to the nature of patriarchy and its intersections.

Race and Ethnicity
Some see the election of Barack Obama as US President as a signal that racism in the US is no longer a problem. However, if your skin color is black or brown, you are much more likely than

a white person to: have a shorter life span; live in poverty; be unemployed; be in prison; drop out of high school; or be stopped or shot by the police. If you are black or brown in the US, you experience racism in everyday life as when you are followed in a store by security staff or when you have to talk to your children about how to deal with the police.

Conservatives generally see claims of racism in the US as exaggerated. Slavery ended over 150 years ago, and, in today's world, they argue that those who work hard can succeed. Indeed, many argue that what we have now is "reverse racism," whereby white people are disadvantaged relative to people of color. They blame liberals and affirmative action policies for leaving them at a disadvantage. Conservatives generally see the Black Lives Matter movement as wrongheaded, unfairly criticizing the police and as not recognizing that all lives should matter equally.

Liberals, on the other hand, seem split. Some support conservative views while others recognize that racial prejudice still exists, that Black Lives Matter is a valid response, and that affirmative action and other policies may be necessary. Most liberals would likely argue that the US has made a lot of progress since the civil rights movement and that electing Obama was emblematic of that progress.

Progressives see racism as still virulent in the US. They recognize progress. Slavery ended, and the civil rights movement eliminated apartheid-like Jim Crow laws that discriminated against people of color in multiple ways. But progressives recognize that this history is still relevant. Slavery began in the US over 400 years ago, and centuries of slavery followed by discriminatory laws characterize most of US history apart from the last few decades. Krugman argues "we are still haunted by our nation's original sin."[166] Racism is seen as more than individual prejudice and bias but as built into and still present in the very institutions and structures of our society. Recent

State legislation that makes it harder for people of color to vote is an example, as is a history of federal government support of housing segregation.[167]

Another example is the US Supreme Court's rejection of affirmative action policies in favor of "color blindness." Chief Justice John Roberts spoke for conservatives (and some liberals) when he said: "the way to stop discriminating on the basis of race is to stop discriminating on the basis of race." Justice Sonia Sotomayor, in defense of affirmative action, counters: "the way to stop discriminating on the basis of race is to speak openly and candidly on the subject of race, and to apply the Constitution with eyes open to the unfortunate effects of centuries of racial discrimination."[168]

Of course, racism is not restricted to the US Racism; it was rampant in colonialism. European colonizers viewed indigenous populations as inferior. This led to slavery, institutionalized discrimination, and even genocide. The "White Man's Burden" saw colonialism as a civilizing force for "savage" natives. So-called "scientific" racism developed a hierarchy of intelligence and morality with white men at the top. "Orientalism" posited the East as inferior to the West. This is not ancient history. And modern history is replete with racism around the world evidenced in Nazism, Apartheid, and recent ethnic conflicts in Rwanda, Serbia, and Kenya. And ancient history is, of course, equally problematic. To the Romans, foreigners were barbarians they had every right to enslave.

Where such prejudices and racism come from is not clear. Some argue xenophobia and "othering" of those different from some "us" is built into the human species. Regardless of whether this is true, progressives believe that it can be overcome, even though that is not easy. US legal scholar Stephanie Wildman wrote: "I simply believe that no matter how hard I work at not being racist, I still am. Because part of racism is systemic, I benefit from the privilege that I am struggling to see."[169] This is not about feeling guilty – and it applies as much to sexism as racism. It is an acknowledgment that the structures in which we live have an impact on all of us. That doesn't mean we can't look at our own racism (or sexism) and diminish it. Bell hooks writes of the need for self-interrogation, deeply questioning our own values, beliefs, and behavior.[170] As progressives, we can ally ourselves with those fighting racism.

For progressives, the struggle against racism needs to be aligned with its intersection with other oppressive structures. Long-term, noted African-American scholars, public intellectuals and activists like Angela Davis, bell hooks, and Cornel West write and speak of the need for linking the struggle against racism with the struggles against capitalism, patriarchy, and heterosexism.[171] Bell hooks writes about the "imperialist white supremacist capitalist patriarchy." She says: "We can't begin to understand the nature of domination if we don't understand how these structures connect with one another."[172] What this means for progressive practice I will return to in the concluding chapter.

I conclude this section with two illustrations of such intersections. One is from the US; Krugman argues that we don't have a more liberal version of capitalism in the US – like the social welfare regimes in Western Europe – because the US is still such a racist society.[173] Southern states – that once practiced slavery – have moved to the Republican Party because racism is more accepted there. They vote against "programs that help the needy" because they "are all too often seen as programs that help 'Those People.'" As an example, Krugman points out that it is, by and large, only the Southern states that refused to expand Medicaid even though it was subsidized by the federal government.

Harvard University's Alejandro de la Fuente wrote an interesting piece for the *New York Times* entitled "A Lesson from Cuba on Race."[174] Despite having an authoritarian political system, Cuba did implement some sort of socialism that benefited Afro-Cubans – mostly descendants from slaves – tremendously. In today's Cuba, life expectancy for blacks and whites is relatively equal, as are high school graduation rates and employment in professional occupations. And this is not because levels are so low; Cuba, on all these measures, does much better than other Latin American countries. De la Fuente does not paint Cuba as a "socialist paradise" – it has "profound problems," but it "advanced a great deal, dismantling key pillars of inequality and providing more or less egalitarian access to education, health, employment and recreation." Nonetheless, his main concluding point is that despite more equal economic progress, racist attitudes are still widespread in Cuba, so that dismantling the inequalities of capitalism is no cure for racism. I think that the lesson for progressives is that structures of oppression are very resistant to change and that changing one does not change them all.

LGBT Issues

LGBT is often used to refer to the lesbian, gay, bisexual, and transgender community. This already represents the intersections of different identities, but the issue is complex. Sometimes LGBTI, LGBTQ, or even LGBTQQI are used where "I" stands for those who identify as intersex and the "Qs" stand for those who identify as queer or questioning their sexual identity. "Gay" sometimes just refers to homosexual men and sometimes to the whole community. Nomenclature is not a trivial issue since it reflects feelings of inclusion and exclusion. Here, I will use the terms "LGBT," "gay," and "homosexual" as inclusive of all those with non-heterosexual identities, despite recognizing the inadequacies of all three terms. I agree with Sherry Wolf that sexuality is "a fluid – not fixed phenomenon… There are not two kinds of people in the world, gay and straight. As far as biologists can tell there is only one human race with a multiplicity of sexual possibilities that can be either frustrated or liberated, depending on the way society is organized.[175]

Historically, there is a record of homosexuality for thousands of years. I think it likely that human beings have engaged in homosexual behavior since our beginnings. At times, such behavior was accepted, as in ancient Greece; at other times, it was proscribed. Patriarchal religions made it a sin, although, even so, it was often tolerated. Some historians argue that while prior to the advent of capitalism there was, of course, homosexual behavior, people, by and large, were not identified as homosexual. Capitalism brought about wage labor through which people could live apart from patriarchal families and choose a non-conforming sexual identity.[176]

In the US, the modern struggle for gay rights is often dated to 1969 and the Stonewall riots, alternatively called an uprising or rebellion, in New York City.[177] Prior to 1969, being homosexual was not on the table as a social issue. The American Psychiatric Association officially listed homosexuality as a disorder. Gays were discriminated against on multiple fronts, could not be openly gay for fear of repercussions, including violence. Men and women were actually arrested even for simply dressing in clothes of the opposite sex. Gay bars were illegal and subject to frequent police raids, and gay people were subject to police brutality. At the Stonewall Inn, a gay bar, a police raid resulted in 3 days of demonstrations and rioting, garnering a lot of media attention. Spurred by the civil rights and women's movements, within the space of a few years, a movement for gay liberation was born across the country. In 1970, on the first anniversary of the Stonewall uprising, the first Gay Pride parades were held in New York, Chicago, and Los Angeles.

In the almost 50 years since then, there have been many significant changes. In most states, laws banning homosexual acts have been repealed; it is now legal for gay people to work for the federal government; there are anti-discrimination laws governing private employment; discrimination in housing is prohibited; barriers to child custody and adoption have been eased; serving in the military is no longer prohibited (until Trump's change of policy for transgender people); and the right to gay marriage was upheld by the Supreme Court.

How these changes are viewed depends on your perspective. Let me start by looking at the perspective of those outside the LGBT movement for gay rights. Conservatives, for the most part, have fought against all these changes and continue to do so. Usually based on religious views of homosexuality as a sin, conservatives are opposed to anything that they see as threatening to the heterosexual family unit. Some conservatives might be in favor of non-discrimination in employment, but most are united against gay marriage. Too often they see homosexuality as an illness to be "cured." As gay rights gets greater visibility, some of these attitudes are changing.

Liberals have been more supportive of gay rights, but with qualifications. While long supportive of non-discrimination in employment, they have waffled on social issues. It was President Clinton who gave the US the "Don't Ask, Don't Tell" policy in the military. Both Clintons and President Obama were initially opposed to marriage equality. The gay rights movement has and continues to change attitudes, helping to make getting the "gay vote" something for politicians to consider.

Progressives, as I have been using the term, generally have been supportive of gay rights. However, I want to qualify this in two ways. First, as a progressive, I can be and am supportive of liberation movements that don't challenge capitalism or other oppressive structures directly. So, for example, LGBT equality in marriage or military service doesn't offer any real challenge to capitalism, but it offers genuine and needed improvements in people's lives. They are part of the struggle against injustice. Similarly, I and most progressives support affirmative action, or efforts by feminists to pass an Equal Rights Amendment, even though none of those really challenge underlying capitalist structures. Second, it is important to acknowledge that there are those on the left who are homophobic, just as there are some who are sexist or racist. I would not consider them progressives, but they are a fact of life, and they generate reaction within the gay rights movement, as they did and do in feminist and anti-racist movements.

Looking within the LGBT rights movement, there are many complexities that I am not qualified to treat well. But I want to point out some that are relevant to progressive, intersectional perspectives. There are a number of distinct lesbian feminist views, all having in common the need to add an explicitly lesbian feminist perspective to both male gay liberation efforts and to liberal feminists' efforts. In the early 1970s, the National Organization of Women actually tried to exclude lesbians, although that was short-lived. There are also groups of lesbian feminists of color such as black lesbian feminists who try to add a lesbian perspective to that of black feminists.[178]

Many black feminists see class and capitalism as important as well as race and gender. Barbara Smith sees black lesbian feminism as "a movement committed to fighting sexual, racial, economic and heterosexist oppression, not to mention one which opposes imperialism, anti-Semitism, the oppressions visited upon the physically disabled, the old and the young, at the same time that it challenges militarism and imminent nuclear destruction..."[179] You don't have to be a lesbian feminist to be concerned with the intersection of gay rights with capitalism and other oppressive structures. Since the founding of gay rights movements, there has long been a leftist perspective present. Peter Drucker's book, *Warped: Gay Normality and Queer Anti-Capitalism*, traces through some of that history.[180] Drucker argues that the gay rights movement "need[s] to give overturning neoliberalism and its gender and sexual dimensions pride of place in our conception of sexual liberation" and that "queer radicalism" needs to define "itself as not only anti-neoliberal, but also anti-capitalist."[181]

Modern-day capitalism has a checkered history with gay rights. For a long time, the movement was resisted, wanting to preserve the ability of business to exclude gay people from employment. However, gay activism has brought on the LGBT community as a new market and made widespread employment discrimination impractical and self-defeating. *The Economist* magazine and some major multinational companies even sponsored a conference in 2017 called "Pride and Prejudice: The Business Case for LGBT Diversity and Inclusion." It was held simultaneously in New York, London, and Hong Kong with "over 200 leaders from the worlds of business, politics, and society to address LGBT issues head-on and bring the debate forward." There are discussions of "Pink Economics," which is basically marketing goods and services to the gay community.

I have talked about LGBT issues in the US. I don't know much about issues worldwide other than, while there has been legal progress, gay people face discrimination in most, if not all, countries and, in many countries, being gay or engaging in same-sex activities is criminal. A few countries even put people to death for being gay. I was working in Uganda, which at one time was considering such a law, and remember well a discussion I had with a black Ugandan colleague, a teacher, who on other issues was very liberal. But she was convinced that gay relations should be criminalized. Her basis for this was her religious beliefs. I tried to liken it to the persecution of Blacks in the US or Apartheid in South Africa or Nazism in Germany. I think she changed her stance a little, but such prejudices are deep-seated and embodied in legal, institutional, and religious structures throughout the world.

Disability

The US Census Bureau reported that about 1 in 5 people have a disability, that is, about 57 million people, and more than

113

half considered it severe. Only about 40 percent of those with disabilities are employed, compared to 80 percent of those without disabilities, pay and benefits are much lower, and poverty rates are almost three times as high.[182] Language, as always, matters. People with disabilities have been called retarded, defective, crippled, or handicapped. The term "disabled people" has been criticized as using the label to define the person, so many prefer "people with disabilities." Instead of seeing disability as a deficit, disability can be seen more as a difference. Sometimes the term "differently abled" is used. "Ableism" is often used by disability rights activists to describe the set of prejudices and practices that devalue people who have physical, mental, or developmental disabilities. Ableism is sometimes defined more radically by progressives as "the systematic oppression of a group of people because of what they can or cannot do with their bodies or minds."[183]

A medical model of disability emphasizes disability as an impairment and focuses on interventions that reduce the severity of the impairment, such as hearing implants. A more social model of disability does not deny functional limitations but sees them as operating within an environment that can be changed by ameliorative policies to overcome barriers to functioning, such as providing sign language translators. From this perspective, "disability is imposed on top of...impairments by the way...[persons with disabilities] are unnecessarily isolated and excluded from full participation in society...[I]t is society which disables persons with impairment."[184]

Disability politics is complicated. Conservative beliefs in individualism and personal responsibility puts at least some of the responsibility for dealing with disabilities on those who have them and their families. Liberals' belief in the need for government intervention to provide greater equality of opportunity places significant responsibility on public policy. However, both conservatives and liberals have come together at times to pass relevant legislation. Perhaps most significant was the 1990 Americans with Disabilities Act (ADA) which outlawed discrimination and required providing access. The ADA's four goals of equality of opportunity, full participation, independent living, and economic self-sufficiency had appeal for both conservatives and liberals.

Progressives often point to a connected history of discrimination, marginalization, and oppression. Slavery was justified by beliefs in racial inferiority. In the early 1900s, wave after wave of immigrants were declared "feeble-minded." The eugenics movement viewed disabilities as deficits that needed to be eliminated from the gene pool, with tens of thousands of people subject to forced sterilizations. The Nazis killed hundreds of thousands of people with disabilities in the Holocaust. Today, progressives view ableism as institutionalized discrimination and highlight its connection with other areas:

Ableism is further compounded by factors like gender, queerness, race, class, age, and colonialism, among other oppressions. It must be part of any conversation regarding intersectionality...[185]

Disability rights activists have criticized conservatives, liberals, and progressives for not understanding some of the positions that they take. One example is the very controversial issue of assisted suicide. In the US, the cases of Elizabeth Bouveia in the 1980s and Terri Schiavo in the 1990s and 2000s were used by many disability rights activists to raise questions about whether approval of assisted suicide is based on a "better dead than disabled" prejudice. Similar issues are raised by prenatal screening that has resulted in over 90 percent of fetuses with Down syndrome being aborted. This disability-selective abortion has been compared with sex-selective abortion of female fetuses.[186] It is not that there is a uniform anti-abortion or anti-euthanasia position by people with disabilities, but there is a widespread belief that people without disabilities don't grapple with these issues.

There is some alliance between conservatives and disability rights activists because of these views on assisted suicide and abortion, but conservatives are criticized for cutting expenditures needed to enforce legislation like the ADA as was Donald Trump's appalling mockery of a reporter with disabilities. Liberals and progressives are criticized for not seeing disability as a civil rights issue. And while progressives may talk about marginalization and oppression, they often hold meetings in inaccessible locations and don't turn out to protest against disability discrimination.[187]

In an article entitled "Capitalism and Disability," Marta Russell and Ravi Malhotra offer a progressive analysis. With the advent of the Industrial Revolution, people with disabilities were forced to compete in the labor market for wages, but could not, and were either neglected or increasingly forced into "workhouses, asylums, prisons, colonies and special schools."[188] The advent of a Welfare State has provided some support (like the ADA), but benefits are low and constantly threatened. Russell and Malhotra argue that a radical disabilities perspective would question a structure where "work is the defining quality of our worth."[189] Although made in a different context, the comments of an American Indian Creek elder are relevant: "We don't waste people the way white society does. Every person has their gift."[190]

Disability is, of course, a global problem. In many countries, the situation is much worse than in the US. Of the 260 million children and youth in the world who aren't in school, a large proportion have disabilities, kept home by prejudices and hostile school environments. The Convention on the Rights of Persons with Disabilities was adopted by the United Nations in 2006, offering international protections. While enforcement is often weak, it has been approved by 172 countries. The United States is not one of them due to concerns about its impact on businesses.

Chapter 10

Other Major Issues

In this chapter, I discuss progressive, conservative, and liberal views of three major issues: health care, the environment, and war and peace. Each could be and has been the subject of many books, articles, op eds, and debates. Here, I will just hit some of the highlights.

Health Care

The health care system in the US is the subject of hot debate. The problems and status of health and health care in the US are appalling. A 2014 study reported:

> Despite having the most expensive health care system, the United States ranks last overall among 11 industrialized countries on measures of health system quality, efficiency, access to care, equity, and healthy lives, according to a new Commonwealth Fund report. The other countries included in the study were Australia, Canada, France, Germany, the Netherlands, New Zealand, Norway, Sweden, Switzerland, and the United Kingdom. While there is room for improvement in every country, the US stands out for having the highest costs and lowest performance—the US spent $8,508 per person on health care in 2011, compared with $3,406 in the United Kingdom, which ranked first overall.[191]

Of the 35 wealthy nations belonging to the Organization for Economic Co-operation and Development, the US is the only country without universal health coverage. Among these 35 countries, the US ranks twenty-ninth in infant mortality and twenty-sixth in life expectancy.[192] Tens of thousands of people die each year because of lack of adequate health care. Almost 40 percent of adults report that they didn't take a treatment, test, or follow-up appointment because of costs.[193] Millions of people are uninsured, many can't afford to go to a doctor if they are sick. Public health clinics and emergency rooms, especially in inner cities, are over-crowded and under-staffed, offering very inadequate care at best.

What to do, as always, depends on your perspective. Many conservatives, before the Affordable Care Act (ACA, also known as Obamacare) was passed in 2010 did not see health care as a major problem, despite that then there were 37 million Americans uninsured. It was the Democrats who passed Obamacare and then conservatives spent the next 9 years trying to repeal it. Among other things, conservatives didn't like its mandate for individuals to get insurance and its provisions to subsidize mental health, contraception, and assistance for poorer families. They also have been critical of Medicaid (health care for the poor) and Medicare (for the elderly) as expensive entitlements. More generally, conservatives have opposed all these programs as unnecessary government intrusion in the market.

Conservative solutions are not too clear as we saw in the difficulty they had in coming up with a plan to replace Obamacare. More radical conservatives want to get the government out of the business of health care almost entirely and leave things to patients and their doctors. Prices for medical services and success rates would be available to make the market work efficiently. They might replace Medicare and Medicaid with individual health savings plans, perhaps subsidized for the poor, and eliminate the tax break for employers who contribute to providing health insurance. Alternatively, they would turn these programs over to the states to fund.

Many liberals and all progressives find these recommendations abhorrent, leading to even much greater inequality in health care access than we have today. Turning things over to the states will yield a chaotic patchwork of programs and policies and even greater complexity and inequality. Liberals want a number of relatively small changes to make Obamacare work better. Some liberals and almost all progressives see the need for universal, government-managed health care.

For progressives, relying on the profit motive is no way to organize health care. Bill Maher, the political commentator and comedian, in an article entitled "Health Care Problem Isn't Socialism, It's Capitalism," opines:

> In the US today, three giant conglomerates own close to 600 hospitals and other health care facilities. They're not hospitals anymore; they're Jiffy Lubes with bedpans. America's largest hospital chain, HCA, was founded by the family of Bill Frist, who perfectly represents the Republican attitude toward health care: it's not a right, it's a racket. The more people who get sick and need medicine, the higher their profit margins.[194]

Health care is almost a $3 trillion industry, and pharmaceutical companies, health insurers, and corporate hospitals are making huge profits. Big Pharma is restricting drug development, spending way more on marketing than on R&D, and charging excessive amounts. Insurance companies routinely deny needed medical treatments and make doctors' lives miserable with endless paperwork. The incentives for doctors to provide good care are all wrong; they get more money the more procedures they recommend. We need to get rid of health insurance companies and substitute a single-payer system. We already have that for the poor and the elderly with Medicaid and Medicare, and they function relatively well. Conservatives emphasize the freedom to choose, but that has just led to great inequalities, and moving health care to even greater individual choice in the marketplace will lead to even greater inequalities. What about the freedom from the worry and stress caused by not knowing if you will be able to get medical care when you need it? Moreover, with a single-payer plan, individuals can still choose their doctors.

My own health insurance comes from my employer, and I didn't have a lot of choice of plans. But my daughter's family were covered under Obamacare, and there was a confusing and complex array of choices to make. Affordable prices, even with subsidies, required choosing plans with huge deductibles. Families can't predict their future, so picking an insurance plan is guesswork. Relying even more on the market and individual choice is an awful idea. You can't go shopping around for medical care when you are ill or have an emergency. Health care is a human right, and we should all have the security of knowing that quality care is available and accessible when we need it.

Leaving aside the US and other wealthy countries, the state of health and health care in developing countries is much more problematic than here. While examining this is beyond the scope of this book, data comparing health status in Europe vs. Africa show that in Africa the maternal mortality rate is 33 times as high, the under-5 mortality rate is 8 times as high, and life expectancy is 17 years less. Fully one-third of children in Africa exhibit stunting from malnutrition.[195] These statistics reflect the global human tragedy that shapes the daily life of poor people throughout the developing world.

Health care was included as a human right in the UN Universal Declaration of Human Rights in 1948. International attention has been focused on health care in many ways in recent decades. In 1978, the World Health Organization (WHO) and UNICEF sponsored an international conference that led to a global Health for All initiative, prior to but similar in ways to the Education for All initiative discussed earlier in Chapter 3. The focus was on accessible primary health care in developing countries to reach the entire population. However, the reality of the past 4 decades is that the 1978 goals have not been achieved.

Progressive critics argue that "the principal culprit in causing growing health inequality is the relinquishment of formerly public administrative responsibilities to market forces."[196] Colin Leys, elaborates:

> In many if not most developing countries the publicly-funded and provided healthcare systems set up after 1945 have atrophied, giving way to private, unregulated and dangerous services, so that in some areas the health gains of earlier years have been reversed. The WHO reported in 2008 that…"small-scale unregulated fee-for-service health care… now dominates the healthcare landscape from sub-Saharan Africa to the transitional economies in Asia or Europe."[197]

The result is a dual system: "a public one – derelict, short of staff, funds and infrastructure – for the poor who also lacked access to the determinants of health; and a private one for those who could afford to pay."[198]

There are several interrelated reasons for this growing global inequality. One is that WHO has been sidelined, especially its work on primary health care systems. As was the case with UNESCO in education, WHO's budget has been minimal considering the challenges it faced. Its efforts have been consistently undermined by corporate interests in tobacco, alcohol, pharmaceuticals, infant foods, and elsewhere.[199]As in education, the World Bank became the lead global organization in public health and aggressively promoted private fee-for-service health care in its loans and their conditionalities. Their neoliberal economics perspective led them and the IMF to promote Structural Adjustment Programs (SAPs) and their equivalent in the 1980s and 1990s which forced developing countries to severely curtail their expenditures on public health.

International efforts by the World Bank and others, including foundations like Gates, became focused on specific diseases, like HIV/AIDS, malaria, and tuberculosis, which while valuable, have ignored supporting public health systems and resulted in the continuing horrendous health situation outlined above. Health care is a global disgrace – as is the poverty with which it is associated.

The Environment

The world population is 7.5 billion. It has almost doubled since 1970. By 2050, it is projected to reach close to 10 billion. Industrial activity and increasing consumption have put intensifying pressure on the environment. According to most scientists, the planet is facing a crisis of sustainability along multiple dimensions. Global warming may well be the most serious and immediate. Global warming is tied to increasing pollution of our air, water, and soil. We are rapidly losing much of our biodiversity with the wholesale extinction of many species. Rampant consumption has yielded an enormous problem of how to dispose of our waste products from plastic to nuclear. Our forests, essential to producing the oxygen necessary for us to breathe, are being cleared. Ocean acidity is increasing.[200]

All of these environmental problems are interrelated and threaten the sustainability of life on Earth. Climate change may be the most immediately threatening. According to many scientists and by general international consensus, embodied in the 2015 Paris Agreement, we need to keep global warming to no more than 2°C. Greater warming may be devastating. The World Bank has warned that:

we're on track for a 4°C warmer world [by century's end] marked by extreme heat waves, declining global food stocks, loss of ecosystems and biodiversity, and life-threatening sea level rise [and] there is no certainty that adaptation to a 4°C world is possible.[201]

This is even more chilling because we don't know how far along the path to global warming we really are. It is worth quoting the 2014 report of the American Association for the Advancement of Science at some length:

> Most projections of climate change presume that the future changes – greenhouse gas emissions, temperature increases and effects such as sea level rise – will happen incrementally. A given amount of emission will lead to a given amount of temperature increase that will lead to a given amount of smooth incremental sea level rise. However, the geological record for the climate reflects instances where a relatively small change in one element of climate led to abrupt changes in the system as a whole. In other words, pushing global temperatures past certain thresholds could trigger abrupt, unpredictable and potentially irreversible changes that have massively disruptive and large-scale impacts. At that point, even if we do not add any additional CO_2 to the atmosphere, potentially unstoppable processes are set in motion.[202]

The idea of reaching a "tipping point" after which environmental disasters spiral out of control is frightening. In my view, we are simply too ignorant to understand very well the complexities of the ecology of the planet. This is why we cannot predict relatively simple complex phenomenon like earthquakes or hurricane paths, much less the intricate balance of all the Earth's ecological systems together. I worry that climate change, as serious as it is, may just be the most visible manifestation of the multiple depredations we are visiting upon our planet.

What to do about the environment, of course, depends on your perspective. Most everybody wants a clean and healthy world, but we differ in important ways.

Many conservatives simply deny the seriousness of these problems. Despite the fact that, overwhelmingly, 97 percent of climate scientists argue that global warming is serious and caused mostly by human actions,[203] conservatives point to the 3 percent who disagree. Most of the latter are funded by the fossil fuel industry, reminding me of the tiny percentage of researchers who denied for decades that smoking causes cancer, who were funded by the tobacco industry. Conservative views have found a home and spokesperson in Trump who has even argued that global warming is a hoax invented by the Chinese.

Liberals, on the other hand, mostly recognize climate change and other environmental problems as real. A 2016 Pew Research center survey looked at the differences between conservative Republicans and liberal Democrats on climate change.[204] A total of 79 percent of liberals said humans were primarily responsible for climate change; 85 percent of conservatives said they were not while 68 percent of liberals said climate scientists had a good understanding of climate change and it was really happening; only 18 percent of conservatives thought so.

Most conservatives are not alarmed by environmental problems. Many liberals are somewhat alarmed but believe climate change and other environmental problems are amenable to technological and relatively straightforward policy fixes. Carbon taxes are one way of encouraging polluters to limit their emissions. Cap and trade policies do likewise by capping emissions but generating allowances that can be bought and sold to allow some pollution – but you have to pay to pollute. In the US, enough companies lobbied against these fixes that neither has been successful. Conservatives and liberals also generally offer some support for wind, solar, and other alternative energy sources – to the extent that they are "cost-effective."

Progressives, on the other hand, are generally very alarmed by the array of environmental problems we face, especially climate change. Naomi Klein's brilliant 2014 book, *This Changes Everything: Capitalism vs. The Climate*, has been a wake-up manifesto for progressives concerning global warming and, in concluding this section, I will draw on it extensively.[205] For Klein and many progressives like me, the conservatives, at best, have their heads in the sand, and, at worst, think that even if climate change does happen, it won't affect them and don't particularly care about how it might affect others. Liberal solutions are seen as too little, too late and are always watered down by corporate interests.

Klein and many progressives, along with many climate scientists, think we may be close to a number of tipping points and that it is urgent to act boldly, decisively, and immediately. The problems with burning fossil fuels will not be solved with:

a few gentle market mechanisms. It requires heavy-duty interventions: sweeping bans on polluting activities, deep subsidies for green alternatives, pricey penalties for violations, new taxes, new public works programs, [and] reversals of privatization.[206]

Klein points out that such changes are what conservatives fear most about climate change – that it is a cosmic signal that to survive we must fulfill the fantasies of the left and put an end to neoliberalism, or perhaps even capitalism itself. The implications, as Klein sees them, are many:

[T] hrough conversations with others in the growing climate justice movement, I began to see all kinds of ways that climate change could become a catalyzing force for positive change – how it could be the best argument progressives have ever had to demand the rebuilding and reviving of local economies; to reclaim our democracies from corrosive corporate influence; to block harmful new free trade deals and rewrite old ones; to invest in starving public infrastructure like mass transit and affordable housing; to take back ownership of essential services like energy and water; to remake our sick agricultural system into something much healthier; to open borders to migrants whose displacement is linked to climate impacts; to finally respect Indigenous land rights – all of which would help to end grotesque levels of inequality within our nations and between them.[207]

For Klein and many other progressives, climate change isn't an "issue," it's a "civilizational wake-up call."[208] As she says, "our economic system and our planetary system are now at war."[209] Conservatives can't admit that climate change is real or:

they will lose the central ideological battle of our time— whether we need to plan and manage our societies to reflect our goals and values, or whether that task can be left to the magic of the market...[H]ow can you win an argument against government intervention if the very habitability of the planet depends on intervening?[210]

Conservatives therefore argue that the whole thing is a hoax and attack climate scientists as liars. The idea that humans are just a part of nature instead of entitled to dominion and control over nature goes against cherished religious and cultural beliefs. Liberals, who can stomach some government intervention, tout modest market incentives. Some of those who are more alarmed posit mad scientist solutions like terraforming Mars or spewing chemicals into Earth's atmosphere to block the sun's heat. This is dangerous hubris, all in the interests of protecting a system that promotes profits over life. As I quoted Gregory Bateson earlier, a fundamental problem with capitalism is that it is based on maximization, it fetishizes growth and ignores the balance that is necessary in all ecological systems.

Klein, despite her apocalyptic vision, is an optimist, as am I and many other progressives. She sees the intersections of many resistance movements and grassroots activism as yielding progressive change, as I have discussed earlier and will return to in my conclusions. She is hopeful that such activism will move the world toward substantial changes such as financing a Marshall Plan for the Earth. If she and many climate scientists are correct, our very survival could depend on it.

War and Violence

As frightening as is the prospect of environmental catastrophe, it pales a little beside the possibility of nuclear war. Not too long ago, presidents Trump and Kim Jong Un were engaged in a pissing contest that was as terrifying as the Cuban Missile Crisis. I don't know enough about Kim Jong Un to characterize his outlook. Many Americans think he is simply crazy and irrational. Certainly, the awful state of his country indicates someone who cares little for the well-being of his people. But many analysts argue he is perfectly rational and simply into self-preservation and that North Korea – since the Korean War – rightly views the US as a potential aggressor threatening attack and regime change, as it has in other parts of the world.

I have a better understanding of Donald Trump than I do of Kim Jong Un, but still we are all guessing about what Trump really thinks and feels. Scariest in this regard is seeing him as a narcissistic little boy, a bully, who reacts off the top of his head to any perceived slight or threat. His "any-threat-by-Kim-will-be-met-by-fire-and-fury-the-likes-of-which-this-world-has-never-seen" seemed to be a visceral, immediate response without much or any thought as to what that escalation of words would invoke in North Korea. It seems to me that Trump – as evidenced by his many tweets – goes by his immediate gut reaction. In a world where diplomacy is essential and too many little boys have their finger on a nuclear trigger, this seems a recipe for global disaster. Gut reactions are very risky when horrific consequences might follow. Joschka Fischer, former German Foreign Minister, argues:

Today's nuclear threats demand exactly the opposite of "fire and fury." What is needed is level-headedness, rationality, and patient diplomacy.[211]

The fact that Trump would take such a risk – no matter how much credit he gives himself for having a gut feel for how to best negotiate – should be a source of dread for all of us. Things with North Korea have cooled down but they could easily flare up again. Plus confrontations with Russia over Syria and Iran raise a nuclear specter. Nuclear war is our ultimate collective insanity; sanity in an insane world demands that we minimize the risk. Trump may not see it this way. He has long fancied himself as the perfect person to preside over nuclear threats and negotiations, and past utterances may indicate that he sees the use of nuclear weapons as inevitable.[212] With over 16,000 nuclear weapons in the world that may be true, especially given the instability of some leaders and governments, as well as the threat from terrorists. "Mutually Assured Destruction" is an incredibly risky strategy for avoiding nuclear war, subject to misunderstandings and technological failures on a hair trigger. Much better would be to rid the world of nuclear weapons entirely, working toward what some have called "global zero." Even if we manage to get rid of Trump in the 2020 elections, the threat of a nuclear war, or even an error, hangs over the world.

Nuclear war is the most horrific outcome of the violence and war that has long plagued human society. In 2014, there were about 40 armed conflicts in the world, inflicting death and horror on literally millions of people.[213] In this section, I wish to briefly consider whether violence and war are inevitable. This issue does not divide neatly along the lines of political perspectives. Nonetheless, I think most conservatives would argue that human beings, especially men, have innate tendencies toward aggression and violence. I think some, perhaps many, liberals and progressives would agree, but at least some, myself included, would say that such tendencies have been exaggerated.

My reading of the evidence on the extent to which aggression, violence, and war are built into our genetic make-up is that it is debatable. The killing of adults in other species is rare.[214] Anthropologist Richard Wrangham says that humans "belong to a club of species that kill adults at an exceptionally high rate – a small club that includes a few social and territorial carnivores such as wolves, lions and spotted hyenas."[215] Males of many species fight but not to the death. The belief that such lethal violence is part of our genetic make-up rests primarily on studies of chimpanzees, our closest living relatives. Groups of male chimpanzees have been known to attack other groups of chimpanzees and kill some. However, some types of chimpanzees, notably bonobos, do not do so and exhibit markedly little aggressive behavior, perhaps, some hypothesize, because food is less scarce and sex is more frequent.[216] I think it likely that there is the potential for aggression in our make-up, but, as with chimpanzees, there is also the potential for cooperation, altruism, empathy, reconciliation, and conflict resolution.[217] Even anthropologists who argue that violence is in our genetic make-up point out that violence in chimpanzees is "calculated" and not engaged in if the outcome is unlikely to be successful.[218]

Violence and war in human society varies widely. Young males in the US are four times more likely to be killed than in any other industrialized country.[219] Some argue that the US is one of the most war-like societies, having engaged in over 150 conflicts since 1850.[220] An interesting recent study examined data on causes of death in 600 human populations from 50,000 BC to today. They conclude:

While only about 0.3 percent of all mammals die in conflict with members of their own species, that rate is sixfold higher, or about 2 percent, for primates…that lines up with evidence of violence in Paleolithic human remains. The medieval period was a particular killer, with human-on-human violence responsible for 12 percent of recorded deaths. But for the last century, we've been relatively peaceable, killing one another off at a rate of just 1.33 percent worldwide. And in the least violent parts of the world today, we enjoy [sic] homicide rates as low as 0.01 percent.[221]

The twentieth century to me was anything but peaceable, but we beat the lethal violence rate of primates and of our even more war-like and violent past. But what is most striking in the above estimates is the variation in rates of lethal violence, from an average of 1.33 percent to 0.01 percent – this is a difference of over 100 times! This shows that, regardless of what aggression and violence may be "built-in," it is far from controlling or necessary. Similarly, we have a history of war in Western European countries that goes back hundreds of years, yet today, war between countries like the United Kingdom, France, Germany, and Spain is pretty much unthinkable.

The nature vs nurture debate has been taken to extremes by sociobiology's genetic explanations of human behavior (what critics have called "so-so-biology"). I think the great variations across history and cultures show clearly that biology is not destiny. David Barash, a biologist and psychologist, argues:

There is no evidence whatever that human beings who have lived a consistently nonviolent life eventually feel a need to commit mayhem at the behest of their frustrated genes. By the same token there is abundant evidence that at the level of societies, people are quite capable of renouncing war, since numerous societies have done just this.[222]

What is the relationship of war and violence to capitalism?[223] While war and violence existed long before capitalism, capitalism has exacerbated them in a number of ways. Many would point to colonialism as fueled by capitalism. In today's world, making or preparing for war is extremely profitable for many companies who lobby to keep the world's "defense" industry going. Deprivation has long been a cause of violence and war. While deprivation existed long before capitalism, progressives argue that, in today's world, it is finally possible to end severe deprivation, but that is unlikely under capitalism. Poverty can be seen as a form of institutional violence. Moreover, the selfish individualism that capitalism promotes works against the collective, cooperative actions and ethos needed to mitigate war and violence. Nonetheless, the capitalist era has seen a change in perspective on violence, where once it was exalted, now it is deplored (despite still being ever present). The abolition of slavery is one example as is:

> the gradual rejection of exemplary cruelty in judicial punishment: burning, boiling, flaying alive, drawing and quartering and breaking on the rack...fell out of favor.[224]

I think most progressives believe, like I do, that political change can and should be accomplished through nonviolent means,[225] but they can still understand why some on the left resort to violence. The anti-fascist group antifa fought with neo-Nazis in Charlottesville, arguing sometimes "you need violence to protect nonviolence."[226] Riots and civil unrest in US cities reacting to police violence were not an organized response by the left but a result of anger and frustration.[227] The Zapatista movement in Mexico, today seen as a peaceful example of an alternative to neoliberal capitalist development, began as an armed insurrection against the Mexican government. Many would argue that, at times, violence is necessary to transform oppressive structures, as with the American Revolutionary War, the French Revolution, or anti-colonial independence struggles.

There are many other important and related issues that I am not able to deal with here but which need at least a brief comment. If men have a greater genetic disposition to aggression than women – despite the many examples of aggressive and war-oriented women – then more equality between the sexes in terms of education and social and political representation can be helpful. The violence we see in our entertainment, especially for children, and sports are not without consequences for human behavior. Terrorism worldwide is frightening, but is not a result of biology; in large part, it comes from the deprivation, disrespect, and hopelessness that too many people feel. Much comes back to formal and informal education. I remember the line from a song in the musical *South Pacific* – "you have to be taught to hate and fear." The reasons that people are taught to hate and fear need to be confronted and eliminated.

What needs to be done to mitigate war and violence is complex. Far too little is being done now. Too many people believe that nothing can be done. But what is unthinkable at one point in time can change. Slavery was once seen as normal. We need a sea change like that that resulted in the abolition of the slavery movement. I am not at all a starry-eyed Pollyanna, but I believe we can change and we must change. Dr Bernard Lown, co-chair of the International Physicians for the Prevention of Nuclear War, which received the Nobel Prize for peace in 1985, states: "We live in a time when accepting this [war] as inevitable is no longer possible without courting extinction."[228]

David Swanson, in his book *War No More: The Case for Abolition*, has a long list of changes that must happen to do so, which include:

A "good war" must sound to all of us, like it sounds to me, as no more possible than a benevolent rape or philanthropic slaver or virtuous child abuse. "You can no more win a war than you can win an earthquake," said Jeanette Rankin, the heroic congresswoman who voted against US entry into both world wars...We must make war abolition the sort of cause slavery abolition was...We must stop trying to discover a good patriotism, and begin thinking beyond borders. We must abandon nationalism without supposing that we are then somehow obliged to hate our state or city when we fail to encourage our state or city to engage in warfare. We must make a concerted effort to remove nationalism, xenophobia, racism, religious bigotry and US exceptionalism.[229]

I am not a pacifist and there may have been no alternative to fighting the Nazis or going after Osama bin Laden. But I believe that we can live on this planet far more peacefully than we are currently doing. Denuclearization is essential. Foreswearing the use of preemptive strikes is also necessary. No matter what threats are said, first strikes should be off the table. And a mass movement to end all wars may sound very idealistic, but perhaps it is time. Humanity has the potential to transform this planet into an oasis, and we are unfortunately very busy moving in the opposite direction. Swanson and others go on to lay out lots of needed changes in the UN and elsewhere and argue for a global Marshall Plan.[230]

Chapter 11

A Note on Research

Before concluding this book, as someone who has been living most of his life in an environment where research and scholarship are prized, I would like to talk about their limitations in helping us find solutions to all the problems I have discussed up to now. In the world of social science and public policy, it is common to conclude analyses by saying that "more research is needed." This is true regardless of whether the underlying perspectives are conservative, liberal, or progressive – or not acknowledged at all. In fact, the ethos of research is that it can remain unbiased, politically impartial, and provide "objective" evidence as to what policies may be most effective, or cost-effective, in solving any particular social problem.

In terms of the public policies that may be needed, research is called upon to answer myriad and diverse questions: Are more and improved educational investments a good route to increasing the income of individuals and the GNP of nations? Are democratic governments and/or free market policies more conducive to economic growth, less conflict, and other indicators of development than autocratic ones? Does government-managed health care yield a healthier population than relying on the private market? Do voucher systems in education increase student achievement? Are carbon taxes an effective way of tackling global warming? Will individual and corporate tax cuts yield job growth and increased government revenue? Are fiscal or monetary policies best for economic growth and attaining full employment?

These and literally thousands of other public policy questions are continually and extensively (and expensively) studied by researchers. While answering such questions is not expected to resolve the differences in values held by those who adhere to different political perspectives, it is generally believed that such answers can provide "facts" to resolve disputes about the impact of policies favored by those with different perspectives. For example, conservatives, liberals, and progressives disagree about the impact of policies favoring private schools and charter schools – or about government-managed health care vs. a fee-for-service private system. Can research help us resolve these and other questions of potential policy impact?

Most researchers answer that question in the affirmative. I personally am less sanguine. While this is not the place for an extensive discussion of the problems with what is called "impact evaluation," it is important for everyone to consider this question and not simply leave it to abstract debates among experts versed in research methods. I will try to summarize briefly my doubts. Much of impact evaluation is quantitative in nature, trying to find the measurable, causal impact of a public policy on some outcomes of interest.

In order to separate out the impact of one factor from the many factors that can affect an outcome of interest, you need to somehow "control" for those other factors so you can isolate the impact of the one you are interested in. There are two ways that researchers think you can do so: one way is through statistical controls. So, for example, let's say we want to find out whether the use of a common educational software for computers increases student achievement. One may be tempted to simply look at the average test scores of students who use that software vs. those that don't or those that use it less often. But any observed test score differences may be due to lots of factors other than whether a student uses that software: there may be differences in the social and economic background of students, in the amount of homework they do, access to computers and other resources at home and at school, their health, the education and practices of their teachers, the size of their classes, and so forth. In fact, there are dozens of factors that impact a particular student's test scores.

To isolate the impact of one factor, in this example, the use of a particular computer software, through statistical controls, there are three conditions that must hold: you must know *all* the factors that affect the test score outcome you are interested in, you must know the correct way to measure them, and you must know their mathematical interrelationship. These three conditions *never* hold precisely (or even approximately) and, when they don't, the measure you get of the impact of a particular factor is inaccurate. This problematic situation seems to hold for most outcomes of interest. What are the factors that determine an individual's income? A country's GDP? The degree of conflict between two countries or within a country? The health of individuals? I believe that the answers to these questions are simply too complex to model mathematically as many social scientists are wont to do. The assumptions that underlie these statistical control models are simply never met, never even approximated, so, even in theory, these models can't work to isolate and determine the impact of a particular policy or program.

The other reason for my skepticism is that this approach to impact evaluation hasn't worked out in practice either. That is, the literally endless array of statistical studies of program and policy impact have not given us any agreed-upon answers to the types of questions I asked at the beginning of this section. Some researchers find that educational vouchers and privatization policies increase student achievement, and others don't. Some researchers find free trade increases economic growth and reduces conflict, while others don't. Some researchers find that government-managed health care systems improve health, and others don't. And on and on.

In my view, this type of social science research has not been able to resolve any of the disagreements among conservatives, liberals, and progressives about the impact of the public policies favored by these different perspectives. To the contrary, each perspective reports findings from these statistical studies that confirm their policy biases. Earlier, for example, I talked about the World Bank's work in education, and, more generally, in international development. They pretend to be unbiased and objective – but their research and policy recommendations have the same conservative/neoliberal biases that are exhibited by more overtly partisan institutions like the Heritage Foundation, the American Enterprise Institute, or the Cato Institute. And while, given my biases, I often agree with the findings of more progressive organizations like the Economic Policy Institute or the Institute for Policy Studies, I don't think their impact evaluations are any more trustworthy than the others.

The problem is not that quantitative data is useless. Numbers can offer very important descriptors of aspects of our social realities. The problem is that we simply can't use our mechanical mathematical models to separate out the causal impact of a particular factor, policy, or program from what are always very complex and contingent processes. Many social scientists have become statistical virtuosos, but as far as I can tell, these statistical control models have been a dead end both in theory and in practice.[231]

This situation is recognized by some quantitatively-oriented researchers who have been promoting a different approach to impact evaluation – the controlled field experiment. Instead of trying to build a mathematical model of all the relevant factors that influence an outcome of interest in order to separate out the impact of one factor, you set up an experimental situation where two or more "identical" groups are subject to different treatments. If the outcome is different for the two groups, the conclusion is that it was caused by the impact of the treatment. In theory, experiments should work to evaluate impact, but in practice there are lots of problems.

Among these problems are that it is difficult or unethical to experiment with treatments that can have substantial impacts on people's lives. Often, the impacts of programs or policies show up over the long term, and it may be unethical to withhold treatment from one group in order to study some impact on another group. Moreover, when treatments are complex policies or programs, it is very difficult to ascertain *why* they may be having some effect, or whether effects are actually caused by the treatment or may be the result of other differences between groups that were not perfectly controlled for. Over the past decade or two, hundreds of millions of dollars have been spent on these social experiments (as well as on statistical studies), but their results are usually disputed. If they are not disputed, it is usually because there has only been one experiment in one location on a topic in one context. Too often such sparse information is taken as gospel, and policy recommendations are made without much evidence.[232]

My point in this chapter is not to argue against research but to suggest that we must be much more modest in what we think research can accomplish. In recent years, there has been an increasing fetishism with the term "evidence." The call for "evidence-based policy" is ubiquitous accompanied by a call for relying only on "rigorous" methods by which is meant the quantitative statistically-controlled or experimentally-controlled approaches critiqued above. My view is that these methods have and will continue to yield little agreement about impact. We simply don't know how to strip the complex relations of the real world to reveal true causal impact. An educational researcher pointed out that physics would be in very difficult straits if sub-atomic particles had intentions and could move any way they felt like at the moment. This is the world of 7 billion people social scientists are dealing with. In my view, it is simply too complex for our simplistic mathematical models to find causal regularities.[233] The most telling evidence supporting this position

– a position which, as you can imagine, is very unpopular with social scientists – is that we have no agreement in any of the fields I have studied on to what extent what causes what. Conservatives, liberals, and progressives all cite research results they agree with, but that research has done nothing to lessen their disagreements. I do believe quantitative and qualitative data can be very useful for describing the world and opinions about it, but will do little, if anything, to prove one or another view correct. Nonetheless, sensible, modest research efforts can be an integral part of illuminating our debates.

Chapter 12

Conclusions

The world we live in is a very beautiful and bountiful place. I have been very fortunate to travel extensively, to dozens of countries, as well as in the US. My work in education and development has taken me to places of both incredible wealth and devastating deprivation. Everywhere I have been – even in the midst of deprivation – there is much beauty. Incredible natural beauty. And incredible human beings. People who are generous, caring, and welcoming. People with an appreciation of the many joys of life, with a sense of humor, with a love of family and place.

Unfortunately, the world we live in is also an extremely difficult place. So many people – actually billions – live in dire straits. Severe material poverty, conflicts and wars, natural disasters threaten so many people's very survival. These conditions have existed throughout human history. Today, we have added massive environmental destruction and nuclear holocaust to threaten the very survival of all of us. To me – and to many others – it doesn't have to be that way.

Human sensibilities and capabilities have evolved and developed. There is sufficient global economic capacity that no one has to live in severe deprivation. There is sufficient knowledge to avoid environmental destruction and potentially sufficient goodwill and understanding to live together on this planet in peace. Yet we are very far from doing so. Why and what can we do about it?

This book is an attempt to shed some light on these two questions, and, in this conclusion, I want to consider some of the implications of my analysis. In the preceding chapters, I have tried to examine three broad political, social, and economic

141

perspectives that I have called conservative, liberal, and progressive. These perspectives are not all-encompassing, but they are commonly held. As I said in the beginning of this book, all categorization is approximate, useful for discussion, but never a complete or accurate depiction of the world, let alone of the thoughts and sentiments of human beings. No one likes to be put in a box. No one fits exclusively in one or another of these three perspectives. Yet to me – and to many others – they represent a useful approximation of an important part of our diverse views.

While I identify with a progressive perspective, I have tried to be fair to conservative and liberal views. It is too easy to create caricatures – straw persons – easy to dispute and knock down. In my teaching and in my writings over many years, I have tried to give an insider's view of perspectives I disagree with and explain why I disagree. In this book, covering so many subjects in a relatively short space, I am sure many of those with conservative or liberal views will think that I did not do justice to their perspectives, and I recognize that as a fair criticism. My intent has been mostly to explain various aspects of a progressive perspective and how progressives see the world very differently from conservatives or liberals.

I believe most people have good intentions. No one really likes the idea of people suffering from severe material deprivation. No one wants massive environmental destruction, nuclear war, or any war, for that matter. However, conservatives generally seem to feel that there is little that can be done. And/or that some of these problems have been exaggerated. And/or that time or new knowledge will eventually make things better. And/or that, while their own family and community may be of concern, the rest of the country and world is not really their responsibility.

Liberals, on the other hand, generally acknowledge that the problems we face are more severe than conservatives see them. Liberals also generally believe that we must individually and collectively take local, national, and global action in order to ameliorate the most threatening problems.

Progressives agree, although most see the problems we face as more dire and immediate than liberals do. Progressives also differ from liberals in that our problems are not amenable to straightforward policy solutions but are deeply embedded in the very structures that constitute our social fabric. In conclusion, I want to return to look again at the nature of these structures, especially capitalism, and reflect on what we might do in order to survive, to live better, to progress. But first, I want to talk a little about the rise of Trump and the far right in the US and elsewhere.

Trump and the Far Right

As I said at the outset, I would have felt the need to write this book even if Hillary Clinton had won the presidency in 2016. Or even if Bernie Sanders or another progressive wins the 2020 election. This book is about some important aspects of the longer-term struggles we are facing in this nation and on this planet. A democrat in the White House – or even a self-labeled democratic socialist – doesn't obviate the need for careful examination of our differences and a call to move us in more progressive directions.

But the election of Donald Trump – and far-right politicians in other countries – certainly has changed the present context. Trump doesn't fit within the conservative, liberal, progressive trichotomy I have been using. He is certainly not a liberal or progressive, although a few of his policy positions may overlap with theirs. He is certainly not a traditional conservative, although many of his positions concur with theirs. Trump's political position is impossible to pinpoint. What he is from my viewpoint – and that of many others – is a disaster.[234] As many people have said, I find Trump to be self-centered, self-aggrandizing, narcissistic, and paranoid. He seems to be full of prejudices – racist, sexist, homophobic, and ableist. The Trump presidency is truly frightening. He and his Republican enablers have set back the progressive tendencies of past decades. Even more than that, Trump has unleashed a climate of prejudice, bigotry, and hate.

Along with many others, I have been trying to understand how Trump won the 2016 election. Are too many Americans truly what Hillary Clinton's unfortunate remark labeled a "basket of deplorables?" I have told myself that it really can't be that 60 or so million Americans are racist, sexist, homophobes; that a large fraction of Trump supporters are basically good human beings who are frustrated, angry, and afraid of the situation they find themselves in and just wanted a change from politics as usual; that they held their nose at Trump's awful rhetoric and just wanted something different from politics and business as usual. But, as I am writing this, we have had almost 3 full years of Trump's prejudices, hate, incivility, warmongering, and absurdities. The midterm 2018 elections provide some rays of hope but still, close to half of the country continues to express support for him and he is very likely to remain president until at least 2020. That is quite depressing.

Add to that a global perspective where similarly far-right xenophobes with fascist tendencies have made political progress in many countries. It is enough to make some progressives give up in despair of humanity. But fortunately, despite being understandable, I don't think that is the tendency of the majority of progressives. Trump and the global far right have just brought to the fore the long-term struggle we face. Naomi Klein has expressed this very well:

Trump is not a rupture at all, but rather the culmination – the logical end point – of a great many dangerous stories our culture has been telling for a long time. That greed is good. That the market rules. That money is what matters in life. That white men are better than the rest. That the natural world is there for us to pillage. That the vulnerable deserve their fate, and the 1 percent deserve their golden towers. That anything public or commonly held is sinister and not worth protecting. That we are surrounded by danger and should only look after our own. That there is no alternative to any of this.[235]

Klein's point in all her work, my point in this book, and the work of many others is that there are alternatives, there are plenty of alternatives – TAPAS! A decent future for ourselves, our children, for all of humanity depends on advancing the struggle for finding and taking fundamentally different paths, creating new stories and making them a reality.

Capitalism

From a progressive perspective, as I have said, alternatives are not easy to enact. It is not simply a question of acknowledging that current policies are wrongheaded and finding the "right" new policies. The stories Klein mentions above are built into our very structures, in the US and around the globe. We live in a world not only of individual prejudices but where much too often racism, sexism, heterosexism, and ableism are an integral part of cultures, religions, and legal frameworks and policies – a part of the very air we breathe. Some alternatives are easier to imagine than others. While patriarchy, racism, heterosexism, and ableism have long histories, many of us recognize that these are harmful, and many of us can conceive of a world where they no longer hold sway. The same cannot be said for capitalism.

Capitalism, for the most part, is seen as useful, benign, even necessary, perhaps a permanent feature of humanity's future. Capitalism is the subject of Margaret Thatcher's TINA – There is No Alternative. Capitalism has been seen as "the end of history," "the end of ideology." Progressives, as I have defined them, don't. There is no reason to believe that the history of the world's social and economic and political systems is over. There are many reasons, as I have discussed throughout, to believe that this historical evolution shouldn't be over, and here I briefly return to consider some of them.

Capitalism is not "efficient," certainly not as economists have defined efficiency, as I discussed in Chapter 4. The central idea of economics that a market system fulfills people's preferences in some ideal way (economists' idea of Pareto efficiency) is bankrupt in theory and practice. If all that is meant by efficiency is that markets deliver goods and services without overall coordination – as was tried and failed in the former Soviet Union – they do. But this is not a reason for "laissez-faire," i.e., to leave them alone. Highly regulated and circumscribed markets will still deliver goods and services without overall coordination. And markets need to be regulated in many ways – in my view, market-based capitalism is one of the most inefficient systems I can imagine. As I said earlier, how can you call a system efficient, despite how much wealth it produces for some, when it leaves billions of people at its margins, often barely surviving, without rewarding or sustainable livelihoods?

The too-often-believed slogan, "what's good for General Motors (i.e., business) is good for the US, or for the world," is simply nonsense, promoted by those whom business treats relatively well. Too many people have bought into this view as common sense, not just in the US, but worldwide. The most disadvantaged people in the world are seen as a market, the "bottom billions," a source of profit. International development is framed as letting business and markets flourish without undue government interference, especially during the past 4 decades of neoliberalism. Market thinking and values have become a fundamentalist religion.[236] Governments and international development agencies have drunk this Kool-Aid, doing much too little to change the gross poverty and inequality that characterize our country and our world. Even under the liberal capitalism in many places prior to the 1980s, gross poverty and inequality were rampant. This poverty and inequality is a logical consequence of capitalism, not an aberration.

Government interventions, often decried as socialism, can help. Businesses often want this kind of socialism – for themselves. Lee Iacocca, CEO of Chrysler Corporation when it was in great financial difficulties, was reported to have said "socialism for me, capitalism for everyone else" – meaning government should bail Chrysler out but don't help anyone else. This logic was quite prevalent after the 2008 financial crisis in the US when major companies lined up to be bailed out. But, regardless of the position taken on bailing out businesses in difficulty, most progressives – and sometimes many others – see the need for government assistance, especially in times of crisis. In the aftermath of Hurricane Harvey hitting Texas in 2017, Bill Maher, the comedian and political commentator, quipped that, for many people, "suddenly, socialism isn't such a bad idea when you are standing in toxic flood waters."[237]

To me, we are all standing in toxic flood waters! Threatened by nuclear war or smaller violent conflicts, environmental catastrophes, severe deprivation, violation of human rights, poverty, and more. This is why we need to move beyond capitalism. Many people, especially conservatives and some liberals, who read these sentiments will call me, and other like-minded progressives, "communists." This is a silly label, intended to close off discussion. If, by communist is meant the approach taken in the former Soviet Union or in China, almost all progressives today reject those systems. If, by communist is meant the writings of Karl Marx, as I said earlier, he wrote almost nothing on what that might mean.

Some might label progressives as "socialists." This may be accurate for some. If all that is meant by socialism is the basic approach I quoted earlier – exercising "democratic power over the allocation and use of productive resources"[238] – many progressives might agree. But, as discussed in Chapter 7, socialism comes in many forms, both in theory and in practice. I wouldn't call myself a socialist, although I agree with many of the tenets held by people who label themselves democratic socialists, like Bernie Sanders. But democratic socialism is not well-defined. Bernie used Scandinavian countries as exemplars, but many would see them as mostly a more liberal form of capitalism with more attention to government intervention to improve people's welfare. This is necessary but unlikely to be enough to make this world a decent and livable place for all of us.

It is quite interesting that, whatever is meant by socialism, it has increasing resonance in US society.

> Polls conducted in recent years have found that almost a third of Americans prefer socialism to capitalism. Breaking down the results, researchers found that socialism beat capitalism outright — 49 percent to 46 percent – among people in their twenties and absolutely crushed it among African Americans (55 percent to 41 percent) and Latinos (44 percent to 32 percent) of all ages. Socialism also edged out capitalism (43 percent to 39 percent) among low-income people of all ages and races.[239]

For progressives, this should be a source of considerable hope.

What is Needed?

I have neither a crystal ball nor any unique insight into what is needed. I concede that it is possible that a return to a more liberal, social-welfare oriented capitalist system could lead to a much better world. But I doubt it. Liberal capitalism didn't help that much in the past. While capitalism does much to promote individual entrepreneurship, it also has a tendency to bring out some of the worst in people as quotes from Joseph Stiglitz and Lars Syll made clear in Chapter 7. Capitalism has fostered the unfortunate scripts Naomi Klein laid out above.

More sweeping changes than a return to liberal capitalism are needed. To me, most progressives are struggling with what needs to be done to make this world substantially less unequal, less sexist, racist, heterosexist, and ableist, to make it more livable for all of us. Throughout this book, I have suggested changes that progressives argue will help do so. In this section, I offer some additional thoughts on what is needed. I have no blueprints for the future, and, indeed, blueprints have no place in what must be a participatory, democratic, collective struggle to define alternatives and make them a reality. But visions of possible futures are useful to help think about where we might be going, and it is in that spirit that this section and, indeed, this book, have been written.

Transforming Work

Central to any transformation of capitalism is transforming the ways in which we work. In Chapter 3, I talked about the global EFA, Education for All, initiative which now has very ambitious goals – among them, getting all children, around the world, to finish a high-quality primary and secondary education. But I have long argued that we cannot have EFA without JFA, that is, Jobs for All. Without decent jobs, families need children to work inside and outside the home to contribute to household support. Without seeing a world of decent jobs in their future, children and youth often drop out of school. Of course, JFA is not just important to promote education – what capitalism lacks most is the ability to provide decent, sustainable livelihoods for most of the world's population.

Too much work is difficult, precarious, and unrewarding. Too often, work is dangerous to one's physical and mental health. Too often for too many, little remunerative work is even available. It is a travesty to call a system like this efficient or fair. I often think of how we pay pennies a day for a product like sugar which connects to people in developing countries being paid a pittance for back-breaking, health-ruining labor. This is insanity, this is evil. Yet it is passively accepted as normal, as outside our purview, as rational and perhaps inevitable.

Even middle-class jobs in the wealthy West are often problematic. More and more, in today's world, many of these jobs are precarious, uncertain. Too many jobs have been stripped of benefits, like coverage for health care. Many middle-class people are afraid of losing their jobs. Even those with good, secure employment usually work in a very hierarchical structure, where they have little control over anything to do with their work environment. Corporate cultures are determined by "bosses," and the rest of the workers must conform to the vagaries and idiosyncrasies of their bosses to survive.

Why can't workplaces be more conducive to more democratic, participatory relationships? This is the essential transformation many advocates of some form of socialist alternative envision. And, as I discussed in Chapter 7, many of these advocates point to a widespread flourishing of alternative enterprises, even in the United States. Worker-owned and managed firms, urban and rural cooperatives, local government run banks and utilities all can offer a different work experience than competitive corporate capitalism. (Of course, some businesses offer more cooperative, participatory environments.) We need a world where all people have a good daily work life, where they have a voice, where they are treated with respect, where they have respect for the work they do, where the culture of the organization is not imposed from the top. The market, left to its own devices, has not and will not generate such a future.

Transforming Politics

If workplaces should be more participatory, so should politics. The Citizens United decision in the US and previous Supreme Court decisions giving corporations human rights need to be overturned. We need to greatly reduce the influence of money in politics. In this right-wing climate, I worry what havoc might be wreaked if current calls for a Constitutional Convention are heeded. Nonetheless, I don't hold the US Constitution as something sacred – it was written by privileged white men in a very different time. It is interesting to speculate what more progressive forms of government might exist without its constraints.

A parliamentary democracy has some appeal. It greatly increases the influence of minority voices (not always very progressive, of course), instead of a take-it-or-leave-it two-party system. A science-fiction story I once read had people selected at random for a fixed term of public service as local, state, and national representatives – and there were means of insuring that their deliberations and decisions were not bought. I see problems, but it would give new meaning to the idea of government as public service. Abraham Maslow, the famed psychologist, once wrote about government by interlocking therapy-groups. They wouldn't have to be t-groups, but the idea is that everyone participates in group discussions about political choices and select representatives to higher level groups, all the way up to the national level.

It is possible that, in the future, people will have a lot more time to participate in politics. While there have long been unrealized predictions about automation and the end of work, the newer ones, premised on the artificial intelligence (AI) revolution, are stronger than ever. A study by researchers at the University of Oxford argues that worldwide by 2030, 2 *billion* jobs will be automated.[240] Perhaps new ones will be found, but, at some point, basic necessities may be produced without a lot of need for human labor. Within our present capitalist system, this would be a disaster, with billions more people left without livelihoods. To survive it well, we would need a new economics and a new politics. A new economics, where work was shared, perhaps even conceived of very differently, and a new politics of equitable distribution of what is produced.

Consider what could happen in the US if somehow we were to decide that a lot of jobs people were currently doing were unneeded. If we had a more peaceful world, we could send most of the military home as well as most defense contractors. If we had a less litigious society, we could let half the lawyers go. If we stopped selling sex and other irrelevant attributes of our products, we could send a lot of advertisers home. What I find interesting is that, despite all these people stopping work, the nation would still have the same amount of desired goods and services as before. We could actually continue to pay all these people the same salaries they had before, they could buy the same refrigerators, televisions, etc, as before, no one would have to give up anything really. If we had 2 billion fewer jobs on the planet, this would be true as well if needed economic output were held steady. There could be a lot more time for political participation, for leisure, for creativity – if we had a different and fairer economic system.

While the end of work as we know it is some ways away, we need to consider moving toward other global changes in politics. I know this frightens a lot of people, but we need more global governance. The world is too precarious and interdependent to allow individuals and countries the kind of unbridled freedom that economic and political conservatives seem to crave. The too-often-maligned United Nations is only a start. It needs more resources and more political power. It should be able to tax and spend globally. One tiny first step might be to beef up the UN Office for Disaster Risk Reduction into one that also engages fully in emergency disaster relief. We should have widespread agreement that disaster relief can't always be accomplished by one country, and it should not depend on the uncoordinated largesse of other countries. A UN coordinated emergency relief effort could be of benefit to the whole planet. But this is only a start. The UN should, for example, have the power to put in the resources needed to achieve the 17 Sustainable Development Goals which were adopted in 2015 by all 193 countries in the UN General Assembly.

Perhaps someday, countries will even be considered anachronisms. I certainly value the history and culture of my country and of other countries I have visited. But I also recognize the common humanity I have seen everywhere. We all share certain hopes, desires, sensibilities. We also share common problems. If human beings and our planet are going to survive over the long haul, we need saner and fairer ways of governing our lives together. Being born to an advantaged family in an advantaged country is an accident of birth. It should not make the difference between life and death.

Transforming Ourselves

When I was teaching undergraduates in the 1970s, one of my students brought her visiting cousin to class. He looked like an American football player but had been raised in China and spoke English with a Chinese accent. His American parents had been agricultural and health advisors in China whom Mao let stay after the revolution. He was sent to Chinese village schools and educated in their version of socialism. He described how when making personal decisions he always considered the impact it would have on others in his village. When pressed by my students, he agreed that he didn't always act in their collective interests, but they were always seriously considered.

In today's Western world, too often we only consider the impact of our decisions on ourselves and immediate family. Too often, we have imbibed the idea that self-interest is normal and that individual greed can be good for everybody. Too often, we see violence as a reasonable way to settle problems. Too often, many of us see ourselves as superior to others we know little about. Too often, we have been taught to believe that nature exists to serve our interests. To transform work and politics, we also have to work on transforming ourselves.

In the mid-1970s, I worked on a Club of Rome project called Goals for a Global Society. The Club of Rome is an organization of prominent individuals that looks toward the future of the planet. In 1972, they published their famous *Limits to Growth*,[241] an early sobering look at how the Earth's finite resources cannot support unbridled economic and population growth. The Goals for a Global Society project was a follow-on, intended to cull from world value systems, mostly through looking at major religions, a set of values that could help guide humanity toward a better future. While this was a grandiose endeavor without much payoff, the intent to contribute to a more sensible and sensitive individual is needed.

We have a lot to learn from different ethical and value orientations. I have a colleague, one of whose specializations is Eastern religions and spirituality.[242] Her courses offer students a different way of understanding themselves, humanity, and civilizations. There is a lot of recent attention to indigenous peoples and indigenous knowledge. Sociologist Boaventura de Sousa Santos' important book *Epistemologies of the South* argues that we are losing, ignoring, or destroying indigenous value systems around the world, committing what he calls epistemicide, to the detriment of humanity's future.[243] In some Latin American countries, like Ecuador, the indigenous concept of *buen vivir*, loosely translated as good, balanced living, has been discussed as a national goal to replace economic growth and rampant materialism.[244] In some African countries, the tradition of *Ubuntu* has challenged the materialism of the West.[245]

The belief in endless growth must end. It is very unlikely that the planet can support a population of 7+ billion people all living with today's consumption patterns of those in the West, let alone the 10 billion people forecast for 2050. We need to lessen the ecological footprint of some while increasing the living standards of others. This requires changes in our economic and political institutions, but also changes in us.

Transforming our children's education is one way to make needed changes. The brilliant Brazilian educator Paulo Freire and his many advocates have written extensively about and engaged around the world in developing a different approach to education, as I discussed in Chapter 8. An approach which recognizes the ways in which inequalities are built into our social structures and how, through individual *conscienticization* and collective action, we can challenge the status quo. An education which teaches about and values the views of others different from ourselves can also be transformative. An education in which we meet and work with people who are different from us can also be. It is hard to be prejudiced against a group when you understand their views, their history, and especially know some of their members.

Though very difficult, we probably need to promote dialog with those with whom we disagree. I hardly know any Trump supporters and have never talked with any in any depth. But perhaps more such dialog would be worthwhile. Perhaps even with neo-Nazis. I am not sure I would want to talk with members of either group, especially the latter. But perhaps I should.[246]

How to Get There?

I am sure that not all progressives would agree with all the ideas I put forth in the previous section – or throughout the book. But how do we get to a better future? There is no easy answer, and I don't have a lot to say about it. Individual transformation is part of the picture, but I, like most progressives, believe mostly in the power of collective action. Although I certainly don't advocate it, I understand that some of that action will be violent, like the Zapatistas in Mexico. Even though their revolutions went astray, the actions of the Sandinistas in Nicaragua and Castro's forces in Cuba to overthrow brutal dictators like the Somozas and the

Batistas are understandable and are being and will be repeated in other places. (The implacable and, in part, violent opposition to these revolutions by the United States may be one of the main reasons they did go astray.)

In terms of collective action, I do have hope for the ballot box in countries that have a representative democracy. There have been progressive governments elected in a number of Latin American countries over the past 2 decades. Bernie Sanders' showing in the 2016 US election was remarkable, which indicates that a progressive candidate may even have a chance in the US. Jeremy Corbyn's popularity in the UK is another hopeful sign. But underlying some election successes and underlying progressive change in general, I, like most progressives, place a lot of hope and faith in the power of social movements.

Progressive social movements have probably been responsible for most of the electoral successes mentioned above. Progressive social movements for specific issues have had a remarkable influence in the US and around the globe – the civil rights and racial justice movement, the women's movement, the gay rights movement, the landless movement in Brazil, the Dalit movement in India, the Arab Spring, the anti- or alter-globalization movement, and many others. At a recent conference where I gave a talk on the need for alternative approaches to education and international development, I was asked what my "theory of change" was? How can these needed progressive changes come about? My answer, like that of many progressives, is that we need to forge politically active alliances across these movements – which means alliances across issues and even across countries. Most of these movements deal with issues that are global. We need to network and act both locally and globally. That is why I am so enamored with the World Social Forum (which I was fortunate enough to have attended twice), as I discussed in Chapter 7. It has been a great source of networking across progressive social movements and has promoted both local and global actions.

While I am an optimist, I recognize that things may have to get worse, even a lot worse, before they get better. Trump and the successes of the far right elsewhere are strong evidence of this, but the hope is that it will generate widespread progressive responses. Progressive critics of capitalism often think that the next crisis will be the straw that breaks the camel's back. The Great Depression of the 1930s did usher is some major changes. President Franklin Roosevelt even went so far as to propose an economic bill of rights, but it did not get sufficient support.[247] Progressives had hopes that the financial crisis of the late 2000s would yield more of a fundamental response than it did. But such crises do raise questions for many about the viability and legitimacy of capitalism, and they will re-occur. And, of course, looming environmental crises may usher in major progressive changes – although perhaps too late for many of us. At this point, in discussions of these issues with my class on Alternative Education, Alternative Development, someone usually brings up stories from films and books of alien invasions. In these stories, it is the threat of conflict with people from other planets that unites the people of Earth to recognize their common humanity and common destiny. Hopefully, we will not have to wait for an alien invasion to do so.

Final Thoughts

Although I have long run hopes for a much better world, I am not looking for utopia, certainly not in the short run. I'd settle for sanity. I am very worried about the kind of world my grandsons – and all our children – will inherit. While my grandsons, due to the accident of where they were born, are very fortunate compared to so many, even they may be facing a very dire future. And so many are facing a very dire present. I believe that – if humanity survives – our descendants will look back on today's world as uncivilized. Billions of people barely surviving, war and other forms of violence everywhere, the planet as we know it close to destruction, prejudice and hate rampant – all in a world that could provide beauty and bounty to everyone – will be seen as primitive, unreasonable, even insane. It does not have to be this way!

About the Author

Steven Klees is an economist and professor of international education policy at the University of Maryland. He holds an MA in economics, an MBA, and a PhD in economics and public policy from Stanford University. He has previously held teaching positions at Cornell University, Stanford University, Florida State University, and the Federal University of Rio Grande do Norte, Brazil. Klees was a Fulbright Scholar on two occasions at the Federal University of Bahia, Brazil. He has given talks, short courses, and worked as a consultant on education, health, agricultural, and telecommunications projects in dozens of countries in Africa, Asia, and Latin America for universities, nongovernmental organizations and agencies like UNICEF, UNESCO, USAID, and the World Bank. Klees has co-authored or co-edited four previous books and written dozens of articles, book chapters, op eds, and blogs. He is the former president and Honorary Fellow of the Comparative and International Education Society.

Notes

1   Goldwater (1960, p. 13).

2   Ibid, p. 14, emphasis in the original.

3   Ibid, p. 15.

4   Ibid, p. 21.

5   Ibid, p. 86.

6   Ibid, p. 21.

7   Ibid, p. 22.

8   Ibid, p. 23.

9   Some are more than "wrongheaded." MacLean (2017) paints a chilling picture of the "attempt by the billionaire-backed radical right to undo democratic governance" (p. xvii).

10 And, of course, there are Republicans who would identify themselves as liberal and Democrats who would identify themselves as conservative. Nonetheless, to converse, generalizations are needed.

11 Krugman (2007, pp. 58-9).

12 Again, Krugman was writing this under the Bush administration, before the elections of Obama and Trump. But this question is still valid today.

13 Ibid, p. 59.

14 Ibid, pp. 59-60. Also see MacLean (2017) for the frightening dangers of "organized money" today.

15 As I explain in conclusion, I would be writing this book even with Bernie Sanders as president.

16 Flake's book does not add anything to Goldwater's portrayal of conservatism; its purpose is more to reinvigorate Goldwater's "clarion call" to the nation.

17 While I have no more sympathy for Flake's call for conservatism than I have for Goldwater's, as a Republican Senator, Flake took some courageous stands against his Republican president – despite the contradictory fact that Flake's voting record was very

much in support of Trump's agenda.

18   The Progressive Caucus of the Democratic Party in the US Congress has been around since 1991.

19   I don't call myself a democratic socialist either, but more on that later.

20   "Neoliberalism" is the term used commonly around the world – although it is rare in the US – to characterize economic and political views of the right-wing conservative era that started to dominate in the 1980s.

21   Krugman today, despite self-classification as a liberal, does hold many views I would call progressive.

22   I do not mean to deny that there are divisions among progressives nor that too often factional fighting within the left has been a problem. There are also divisions within conservatives and liberals. Throughout the book, when I use terms like "conservatives see…" or "progressives argue…" I am trying to depict central tendencies.

23   Parts of this chapter were taken, with permission, from Klees (forthcoming).

24   Coleman et al. 1966.

25   Jencks et al., 1975.

26   National Commission on Excellence in Education (1983, p. 9).

27   Carnoy, Rothstein, and Benveniste (2003).

28   CREDO (2013).

29   Malen et al. (2002).

30   Ravitch (2010).

31   Kohn (2000).

32   Klees (2016b).

33   New Public Management is the term used to describe a whole host of changes in the neoliberal era that try to apply narrow versions of business practices to government.

34   Rand Corporation (n.d.).

35   Klees (1994).

36   Ravitch (2010, p. 17). Rather surprisingly, a group of progressive historians at UCLA were funded by a conservative Bush

administration to develop the history standards.

37   Ibid, p. 18.

38   Test scores show that students did no poorer in the 1990s and 2000s than they did in earlier eras; any slight decline in scores was due to many more disadvantaged students taking the tests (Berliner, et al., 2014).

39   Ravitch (2013, p. 16).

40   Spring (2015, pp. 72-3).

41   Reardon (2011).

42   American Institutes for Research (n.d.).

43   See Arnove (2007, p. 393) for a progressive critique: "Although these foundations claim to attack the root causes of the ills of humanity, they essentially engage in ameliorative practices to maintain social and economic systems that generate the very inequalities and injustices they wish to correct." Also see Arnove (1980).

44   See Ravitch (2010, 2013); also see Barkan (2011).

45   Ravitch (2010, p. 217).

46   Barkan (2011).

47   Hess quoted in Ravitch (2010, p. 201).

48   Ravitch (2013, 317-18).

49   Parts of this chapter were taken, with permission, from Klees (forthcoming).

50   The terms "developed" and "developing" are very problematic (Esteva, Babones, and Babcicky, 2013). I still use them for a lack of good alternatives.

51   Sahlberg (2015).

52   Berliner and Glass (2014).

53   Gordon Brown, "Project Syndicate": "A Bridge to Universal Education," April 20, 2017.

54   Klees (2017).

55   Brown (2017).

56   Weiler (1984).

57   Verger, Fontdevila, and Zancajo (2016).

58   Ibid.

59   Macpherson (2014).

60   Klees, Samoff, and Stromquist (2012).

61   Broad (2006).

62   Parts of this chapter were taken, with permission, from Klees (2016a).

63   Rakowski (1980); Friedman (1984).

64   Waring (1988); Daly (1996); Costanza et al. (2009).

65   There are many calls to reform how we measure GNP.

66   Thurow (1983, p. xix). Even relatively mild forms of dissent are often met by disregard, hostility, or derision from neoliberal economists. I remember being struck by George Psacharopoulos telling me that some of his colleagues at the World Bank called Lester Thurow, "Less Thorough."

67   Stiglitz (2013, p. xv). Stiglitz, like Thurow, has been severely criticized by neoliberal economists for his dissenting views.

68   Please remember that putting people in boxes – like neoliberal, liberal, and progressive – are approximations. For example, much of Stiglitz' work is rather progressive (as is Krugman's), but I wouldn't classify either as a political economist in the sense that I have been using the term, and neither would likely agree with the views below.

69   Reinert (2012, p. 2).

70   Fullbrook (2016, p. 2).

71   Fullbrook (2016, p. 135).

72   Amin (1998, p. 14).

73   Amin (1998, pp. 139-40).

74   Parts of this chapter were taken, with permission, from Klees (2016c).

75   https://www.dosomething.org/facts/11-facts-about-hunger-us; http://www.aecf.org/m/resourcedoc/aecf-2017kidscountdata book.pdf; http://www.huffingtonpost.com/2013/09/06/illiteracy-rate_n_3880355.html

76   http://www.aecf.org/m/resourcedoc/aecf-2017kidscountd

atabook.pdf

77   https://www.dosomething.org/us/facts/11-facts-about-global-poverty
78   Holland (2015).
79   This is Reeves' (2017) book subtitle.
80   Long (2017).
81   Piketty (2014, p. 265).
82   Oxfam (2016). Also see Zucman (2017).
83   Astonishingly, in a 700-page book on inequality, Piketty doesn't even mention issues of poverty. For this and my other critiques of Piketty, see Klees (2016c).
84   Wade, 2014, p. 20; *Economist*, 2014; *Financial Times*, 2014.
85   Wade, 2014, p. 17.
86   Foster and Yates, 2014, Kunkel, 2014; Syll, 2014
87   There are some notable recent exceptions of inattention to inequality by liberals. See, e.g., Atkinson (2015); Bourguignon (2015); Milanovic (2016); and Stiglitz (2013).
88   Mishel and Schleder (2017).
89   Quoted in Krugman (2014).
90   Kuznets (1955).
91   Nonetheless, even liberals like Piketty buy into marginal productivity theory to some extent. Piketty just argues that the super-salaries of the rich far exceed their productivity but accepts income differences as reflecting productivity differences for the rest of workers (Klees, 2016c).
92   Stiglitz (2013, p. liii).
93   Inman (2015).
94   Wilkinson and Pickett (2010).
95   Atkinson (2015). Also see Saez and Zucman (forthcoming) who, like Piketty (2014), propose a tax on wealth.
96   Collins (2017).
97   Jolly, Stewart, and Cornia (1987).
98   More on civil society later.
99   See Edwards and Klees (2012) for elaboration.

100 See Klees (2008) for a more detailed discussion.

101 See Klees (2009) for a critical analysis of the language of development.

102 Weiler (1984).

103 Appeared in *Adult Education and Development*, September 1976.

104 See Illich (1968) for a biting look at the paternalism of "helping."

105 Alexander (2015); Bretton Woods Project (2016).

106 Kennard and Provost (2016)

107 Parts of this chapter were taken, with permission, from Klees (forthcoming).

108 Giridharadas (2018, pp. 6-10).

109 Ibid, p. 7.

110 World Economic Forum (2010). Also see Hickel (2015) and Olmedo (2016).

111 Quoted in Wall (2015, p. 1). See Hahnel (2005) for discussion of alternatives to markets.

112 Syll (2014, p. 7).

113 Stiglitz (2013, pp. xlvii-l).

114 Stiglitz (2019) sees the possibility of a "progressive capitalism."

115 Fukuyama (2006)

116 Quoted in Motala and Vally (2014, p. 1).

117 Ibid, p. 16.

118 David Ellerman (2015), formerly an economist at the World Bank, argues that the capitalist system of wage labor, embodied in the employer-employee contract, is, like slavery, based on coercion and calls for a neo-abolitionist movement.

119 Wallerstein (2004).

120 Quoted in Albert (2014, p. xv).

121 Bollier (2015, p. xii).

122 Wright (201, p. 368).

123 Kovel (2014). Also see Daly (1996); Broad and Cavanagh (2009); Klein (2014); and Korten (2015).

124 Wright (2010, p. 369).

125 Albert (2014); Hahnel (2005).

126 Also see Schweikart (2002); Cavanagh and Mander (2004); Wolff (2012).

127 See Alperovitz (2011, 2013). He is one of the organizers of the Next System Project, focused on finding alternatives to current structures (http://thenextsystem.org/).

128 Alperovitz and Albert (2014). See this for an interesting dialog between them.

129 Hahnel (2005); Wright (2010).

130 Ibid. Also see Sandbrook (2014).

131 Satgar (2014); Wall (2015). For a related feminist vision see Gibson-Graham (2006).

132 Esteva, Babones, and Babcicky (2013).

133 Tarlau (2019).

134 Sandbrook (2014); Sousa Santos (2014).

135 Sousa Santos (2008, p. 252).

136 Bello quoted in Sousa Santos (2008, p. 264).

137 Chomsky (2014, p. ix).

138 Reich (2015); Lakey (2016).

139 https://www.goodreads.com/quotes/3238058-we-live-in-capitalism-its-power-seems-inescapable-so-did

140 Parts of this chapter were taken, with permission, from Klees (forthcoming).

141 Gorz (1967).

142 Apple, Au, and Gandin (2009).

143 Ibid, p. 3. Also see Fraser (2005).

144 Kincheloe (2007).

145 Johnstone and Terzakis (2012, p. 197).

146 McLaren (2000, p. 193).

147 Picower (2012, p. 4).

148 May and Sleeter (2010).

149 Guttman (1987).

150 Apple and Beane (2007).

151 Kahn (2010).

152 Hyslop-Margison and Thayer (2009).

153 Picower (2012, p. 4).

154 O'Cadiz, Wong, and Torres (1998).

155 Fischman and Gandin (2007).

156 McGowan (2003); Tarlau (2019).

157 Edwards and Klees (2012).

158 McLaren (2007, p. 310).

159 Baxter (2016).

160 Ibid, p. 27.

161 Each of the theories mentioned has its own traditions and foci, there are important differences within and among them, and, unfortunately, too often, they are quite insular, not communicating with each other.

162 Some use the term "neoconservative" instead but, in the US, this is often associated with views on foreign policy only.

163 Brenner (2014).

164 Smith (2013/14).

165 Herr (2014).

166 Krugman (2015).

167 Rothstein (2017).

168 Quoted in Rothstein (2014).

169 Quoted in Yancy (2015).

170 hooks (2015).

171 See Davis (1983); hooks (2015); West (2005).

172 Yancy and hooks (2015).

173 Krugman (2015).

174 De la Fuente (2013).

175 Wolf (2009, p. 20).

176 D'Emilio and Freedman (1988); D'Emilio (1992); Wolf (2009).

177 The recent fiftieth anniversary of the Stonewall riots were celebrated around the US and elsewhere.

178 Remember, all these and other labels, while useful for some conversations, are problematic.

179 Quoted in Smith (2013-14).

180 Drucker (2015). Also see D'Emilio, op cit., D'Emilio and Freedman,

op cit. and Wolf, op cit.
181 Drucker (2015, pp. 8, 24).
182 US Census Bureau (2012).
183 FWD/Forward (2010).
184 Russell and Malhotra (2002, p. 211).
185 Zaikowski (2016).
186 Ne'eman (2009)
187 Zaikowski, op cit.
188 Russell and Malhotra, op cit, p. 213.
189 Ibid, p. 223
190 Quoted in Wolf, op. cit., p. 23.
191 Commonwealth Fund (2014).
192 Universal Health Foundation (2016).
193 Commonwealth Fund (2014).
194 Maher (2009).
195 World Health Organization (2017).
196 Applbaum (2009, p. 84).
197 Leys (2009, p. 8).
198 Rao (2009, p. 268) is talking about India here but it applied generally to developing countries.
199 Koivusalo (2009, p. 281).
200 Conserve Energy Future (2019); Tercek (2017).
201 Quoted in Klein (2014, p. 13).
202 Quoted in Klein (2014, p. 1).
203 This statistic is from the American Association for the Advancement of Science (quoted in Klein (2014, p. 31)).
204 Funk and Kennedy (2016). The survey separated conservatives and liberals from more moderate Republicans and Democrats.
205 Also see Kovel (2007; Panitch and Leys (2007); Juniper (2014); Roy (2014); Bell (2015); Movahed (2016).
206 Klein (2014, p. 39).
207 Klein (2014, p. 7).
208 Ibid, p. 25.
209 Ibid, p. 21.

210 Ibid, p. 40-42.

211 Fischer (2017).

212 Corn (2017).

213 Gates et al. (2016).

214 Infanticide is more common. See Yong (2016).

215 Quoted in Yong (2016).

216 Horgan (2008)

217 Ibid.

218 Ibid.

219 According to the Journal of the American Medical Association quoted in *Time*, July 9, 1990.

220 Kohn (1988).

221 Engelhaupt (2016).

222 Barash (2014).

223 See Panitch and Leys (2008) for a variety of viewpoints.

224 Bernstein, Leys, and Panitch (2008, p. 12).

225 Fromer (2017).

226 Singer (2017).

227 Ciccariello-Maher (2015) and others argue that riots sometimes "work" to bring needed attention and action.

228 Quoted in Kohn (1988).

229 Swanson (2013).

230 See Shifferd, Hiller, and Swanson (2015) and Horgan (2012).

231 Klees (2016b); Leamer (1983).

232 Deaton and Cartwright (2016); Edwards (2018); Klees (2016b); Pogrow (2017).

233 Berliner (2002).

234 Klein (2017b).

235 Klein (2017a, p. 15).

236 Sandel (2013); Giridharadas (2018).

237 Bill Maher Show, HBO, September 8, 2017.

238 Wright (2010, p. 369).

239 Katch (2015). Although this quote is from a book about socialism, the poll results are from Pew, Rasmussen, and Gallup. Google

"polls socialism capitalism" for more recent confirmation.

240 Frey and Osborne (2013).

241 Meadows et al. (1972).

242 Lin (2006).

243 Sousa Santos (2014).

244 Balch (2013).

245 Flippin (2012).

246 Reich (2018); Headlee (2017); Lesser (2016).

247 Roosevelt (1944/n.d.).

References

Albert, Michael. 2014. *Realizing Hope: Life Beyond Capitalism*. NY: Zed.

Alexander, Nancy. 2015. "The Age of Megaprojects," *Project Syndicate*, July 10. https://www.project-syndicate.org/commentary/g20-infrast ructure-investment-by-nancy-alexander-2015-07

Alperovitz, Gar. 2013. *What Then Must We Do: Straight Talk About the Next American Revolution*. White River Junction, VT: Chelsea Green Publishing.

Alperovitz, Gar. 2011. *America Beyond Capitalism: Reclaiming Our Wealth, Our Liberty & Our Democracy*. Hoboken, NJ: Wiley and Sons.

Alperovitz, Gar and Albert, Michael. 2014. "Gar Alperovitz and Michael Albert: A Conversation on Economic Visions," *Truthout*, March 21. http://truth-out.org/opinion/item/22557-gar-alperovitz-and-michael-albert-a-conversation-on-economic-visions#.Uyxl2kZ7L1k.email

American Institutes for Research. n.d. "Does Money Make a Difference? Connecting Resources to Outcomes." http://www.sedl.org/policy/insights/n14/2.html

Applbaum, Kalman. 2009. "Marketing Global Health Care: The Practices of Big Pharma," in Leo Panitch and Colin Leys (eds.) *Morbid Symptoms: Health Under Capitalism*. NY: Monthly Review Press.

Apple, Michael W., Au, Wayne, and Luis A. Gandin. 2009. "Mapping Critical Education." in Michael W. Apple, Wayne Au, and Luis A. Gandin. eds. *The Routledge International Handbook of Critical Education*. NY: Routledge.

Apple, M. and J. Beane. (eds.) 2007. *Democratic Schools: Lessons in Powerful Education*, 2nd edition. Portsmouth, NH: Heinemann.

Amin, Samir. 1998. *Spectres of Capitalism: A Critique of Current Intellectual Fashions*. NY: Monthly Review Press.

Arnove, Robert. 2007. "Revisiting the 'Big Three' Foundations," *Critical Sociology*, 33: 389-425.

Arnove, Robert. (ed.) 1980. *Philanthropy and Cultural Imperialism: The Foundations at Home and Abroad*. Boston: G.K. Hall.

Atkinson, Anthony. 2015. *Inequality: What Can Be Done?* Cambridge, MA: Harvard University Press.

Balch, Oliver. 2013. *"Buen Vivir*: The Social Philosophy Inspiring Movements in South America," *The Guardian*, February 4. https://www. theguardian.com/sustainable-business/blog/buen-vivir-philosophy-south-america-eduardo-gudynas

Barash, David. 2014. "Are Human Beings Naturally Violent and Warlike?" *Philosophy Now*, 105. https://philosophynow.org/issues/105/Are_Human_Beings_Naturally_Violent_And_Warlike

Barkan, Joanne. 2011 (Winter). "Got Dough? How Billionaires Rule Our Schools." *Dissent*. https://www.dissentmagazine.org/article/got-dough-how-billionaires-rule-our-schools

Baxter, Jorge. 2016. *Who Governs Educational Change? The Paradoxes of State Power and the Pursuit of Educational Reform in Ecuador (2007-2015).* Unpublished doctoral dissertation, University of Maryland, College Park.

Bell, Karen. 2015. "Can the Capitalist Economic System Deliver Environmental Justice," *Environmental Research Letters*, 10 (12), http://iopscience.iop.org/article/10.1088/1748-9326/10/12/125017

Berliner, David. 2002. Educational Research the Hardest Science of All, *Educational Researcher*, 31,8 (November) 18-20.

Berliner, David C., Glass, Gene V. and Associates. 2014. *50 Myths and Lies That Threaten America's Public Schools: The Real Crisis in Education.* NY: Teachers College.

Bernstein, Henry, Leys, Colin, and Panitch, Leo. 2008. "Reflections of Violence Today," in Panitch, Leo and Leys, Colin (eds.) 2008. *Violence Today: Actually Existing Barbarism.* NY: Monthly Review Press.

Bollier, David. 2015. "Foreword to the New Edition." In Derek Wall. *Economics After Capitalism.* London: Pluto.

Bourguignon, Francois. 2015. *The Globalization of Inequality.* Princeton, NJ: Princeton University Press.

Brenner, Joanna. 2014. "Socialist Feminism in the 21st Century," *Solidarity*, March/April. https://solidarity-us.org/atc/169/p4105/

Bretton Woods Project. 2016. "World Bank Rolls Out the Carpet for 'Troubled Megaprojects' and PPPs," April 5. http://www.brettonwoodsproject.org/2016/04/world-bank-rolls-out-the-carpet-for-troubled-megaprojects/

Broad, Robin. (2006, August). "Research, knowledge, and the art of 'paradigm maintenance': the World Bank's development economics vice-presidency." *Review of International Political Economy*, 13(3), 387-419.

Broad, Robin and John Cavanagh. 2009. *Development Redefined: How the Market Met its Match*. Boulder, CO: Paradigm.

Brown, Gordon. 2017. "A Bridge to Universal Education," *Project Syndicate*, April 20, https://www.project-syndicate.org/commentary/universal-education-finance-facility-by-gordon-brown-2017-04

Carnoy, Martin, Rothstein, Richard, and Luis Benveniste. 2003. *All Else Equal: Are Public and Private Schools Different?* NewYork: RoutledgeFalmer.

Cavanagh, John and Jerry Mander. 2004. *Alternatives to Economic Globalization*. Oakland, CA: Berrett-Koehler.

Chomsky, Noam. 2016. *Who Rules the World?* NY: Metropolitan.

Chomsky, Noam. 2014. "Foreword." in Michael Albert. *Realizing Hope: Life Beyond Capitalism*. NY: Zed.

Ciccariello-Maher, George. 2015. "Riots Work: Wolf Blitzer and the Washington Post Completely Missed the Real Lesson from Baltimore," *Salon*, May 4. http://www.salon.com/2015/05/04/riots_work_wolf_blitzer_and_the_washington_post_completely_missed_the_real_lesson_from_baltimore/

Coleman, James et al. 1966. *Equality of Educational Opportunity*. Washington, DC: National Center for Educational Statistics.

Collins, Chuck. 2017. "Reversing Inequality: Unleashing the Transformative Potential of an Equitable Economy," Next System Project, August 3. https://thenextsystem.org/inequality

Commonwealth Fund. 2014. "US Health System Ranks Last Among Eleven Countries on Measures of Access, Equity, Quality, Efficiency, and Healthy Lives," June 16. http://www.commonwealthfund.org/publications/press-releases/2014/jun/us-health-system-ranks-last

Conserve Energy Future. 2019. "Environmental Problems." http://www. conserve-energy-future.com/15-current-environmental-problems.php

Corn, David. 2017. "Trump has Been Thinking about Nuclear War for Decades," *Mother Jones*, August 11. http://www.motherjones.com/ politics/2017/08/trump-has-been-thinking-about-nuclear-war-for- decades-heres-why-thats-scary/

Costanza, Robert, Maureen Hart, Stephen Posner, and John Talberth. 2009. "Beyond GDP: The Need for New Measures of Progress." Frederick S. Pardee Center Working Paper No. 4, Boston University, Boston, MA (January) http://www.oecd.org/site/progresskorea/ globalproject/42613423.pdf

CREDO. 2013. "National Charter School Study." Palo Alto, CA: Stanford University.

Daly, Herman E. 1996. *Beyond Growth: The Economics of Sustainable Development*. Boston: Beacon Press.

Davis, Angela. 1983. *Women, Race and Class*. NY: Random House.

Deaton, Angus and Cartwright, Nancy 2016. "Understanding and Misunderstanding Randomized Controlled Trials," NBER Working Paper No. 22595. http://www.nber.org/papers/w22595

De la Fuente, Alejandro. 2013. "A Lesson from Cuba on Race," *New York Times*, Opinionator, November 17.

D'Emilio, John. 1992. "Capitalism and Gay Identity," In *Making Trouble: Essays on Gay History, Politics and the University*. NY: Routledge.

D'Emilio, John and Estelle Freedman. 1988. *Intimate Matters: A History of Sexuality in America*. NY: Harper and Row.

Drucker, Peter. 2015. *Warped: Gay Normality and Queer Anticapitalism*. Chicago: Haymarket.

Edwards Jr., D. B. (2018). *Global Education Policy, Impact Evaluations, and Alternatives: The Political Economy of Knowledge Production*. New York: Palgrave MacMillan.

Edwards Jr., D. Brent and Steven Klees. 2012. "Participation in Development and Education Governance." In A. Verger, M. Novelli and H. Kosar-Altinyelken (eds.), *Global Education Policy and International Development: New Agendas, Issues and Programmes*. New York: Continuum.

Ellerman, David. 2015. "On the Renting of Persons: The Neo-Abolitionist Case Against Today's Peculiar Institution," *Economic Thought*. 4 (1): 1-20.

Engelhaupt, Erika. 2016. "How Human Violence Stacks Up Against Other Killer Animals," *National Geographic*, September 28. http://news. nationalgeographic.com/2016/09/human-violence-evolution-animals-nature-science/

Esteva, Gustavo, Babones, Salvatore, and Philipp Babcicky. 2013. *The Future of Development: A Radical Manifesto*. Chicago: Policy Press.

Financial Times. Big Questions Hang over Piketty's Work. editorial. May 27.

Fischer, Joschka. 2017. "The New Nuclear Danger," *Project Syndicate*, August 23. https://www.project-syndicate.org/columnist/joschka-fischer

Fischman, Gustavo and Luis Armando Gandin. 2007. "Escola cidade and critical discourses of educational hope." In McLaren, P., Kincheloe, J. L. (Eds.), *Critical Pedagogy: Where Are We Now?* New York: Peter Lang, pp. 209-221.

Flake, Jeff. 2017. *Conscience of a Conservative: A Rejection of Destructive Politics and a Return to Principle*. NY: Random House.

Flippin, William. 2012. "*Ubuntu*: Applying African Philosophy in Building Community," *Huffington Post: The Blog*, February 5. https://www. huffingtonpost.com/reverend-william-e-flippin-jr/ubuntu-applying-african-p_b_1243904.html

Foster, John Bellamy and Michael D. Yates. 2014. "Piketty and the Crisis of Neoclassical Economics." *Monthly Review*, 66, no. 6 (November): 1-24.

Fraser, Nancy. 2005. *Reframing Justice*. Amsterdam: Koninklijke Van Gorkum.

Frey, Christopher and Osborne, Michael. 2013. "The Future of Employment: How Susceptible are Jobs to Computerisation?" University of Oxford. https://www.oxfordmartin.ox.ac.uk/downloads/academic/The_Future_of_Employment.pdf

Friedman, Lee S. 1984. *Microeconomics Policy Analysis*. NY: McGraw-Hill.

Fromer, Yoav. 2017. "Why the Left Gave Up on Political Violence," *Washington Post*, August 20. p B1.

Fukuyama, Francis. 2006. *The End of History and the Last Man*. NY: Simon and Schuster.

Fullbrook, Edward. 2016. *Narrative Fixation in Economics*. London: College Publications.

Funk, Cary and Kennedy, Brian. 2016. "The Politics of Climate," Pew Research Center (October 4) http://www.pewinternet.org/2016/10/04/the-politics-of-climate/

FWD/Forward. 2010. "What is Ableism?" http://disabledfeminists.com/2010/11/19/what-is-ableism-five-things-about-ableism-you-should-know/

Gates, Scott, Nygard, Havard, Strand, Havard, and Henrik Urdal. 2016. "Trends in Armed Conflict, 1946-2014," Peace Research Institute Oslo. http://file.prio.no/publication_files/prio/Gates,%20Nyg%C3%A5rd,%20Strand,%20Urdal%20-%20Trends%20in%20Armed%20Conflict,%20Conflict%20Trends%201-2016.pdf

Gibson-Graham, J. K. 2006. *A Postcapitalist Politics*. Minneapolis: University of Minnesota.

Giridharadas, Anand. 2018. *Winners Take All: The Elite Charade of Changing the World*. NY: Knopf.

Goldwater, Barry. 1960. *The Conscience of a Conservative*. Shepherdsville, KY: Victor Publishing.

Gorz, Andre. 1967. *Strategy for Labor: A Radical Proposal*. Boston: Beacon.

Gutmann, Amy. 1987. *Democratic Education*. Princeton, NJ: Princeton University.

Hahnel, Robin. 2005. *Economic Justice and Democracy: From Competition to Cooperation*. NY: Routledge Press.

Hanushek, Eric. 1981. Throwing Money at Schools. *Journal of Policy Analysis and Management*, 1(1), 19-41.

Headlee, Celeste. 2017. *We Need to Talk*. NY: Harper Wave.

Herr, Ranjoo Seodu. 2014. "Reclaiming Third World Feminism: Or Why Transnational Feminism Needs Third World Feminism," *Meridians*, 12, 1, 1-30.

Hickel, Jason. 2015. "The Problem with Saving the World: The UN's new SDGs Aim to Save the World Without Transforming it." *Jacobin*. https://

www.jacobinmag.com/2015/08/global-poverty-climate-change-sdgs/?utm_campaign=shareaholic&utm_medium=facebook&utm_source=socialnetwork

Holland, Joshua. 2015. "20 People Now Own as Much Wealth as Half of all Americans," *The Nation*, December 3.

hooks, bell. 2015. *Feminism is for Everybody: Passionate Politics*. NY: Routledge.

Horgan, John. 2008. "Has Science Found a Way to End All Wars?" *Discover*, March 13. http://discovermagazine.com/2008/apr/13-science-says-war-is-over-now

Horgan, John. 2012. *The End of War*. McSweeny.

Hyslop-Margison, Emery J. and James Thayer. 2009. *Teaching Democracy: Citizenship Education as Critical Pedagogy*. Rotterdam: Sense.

Illich, Ivan. 1968. "To Hell with Good Intentions," Talk to the Conference on InterAmerican Student Projects, Cuenavaca, Mexico, April 20. http://www.swaraj.org/illich_hell.htm

Inman, Phillip. 2014. "IMF Study Finds Inequality is Damaging to Economic Growth," *The Guardian*, February 26. https://www.theguardian.com/business/2014/feb/26/imf-inequality-economic-growth

Jencks, Christopher et al. 1975. *Inequality: A Reassessment of the Effect of Family and Schooling in America*. NY: Penguin.

Johnstone, Adrienne and Elizabeth Terzakis. 2012. "Pedagogy and Revolution: Reading Freire in Context," in Jeff Bale and Sarah Knopp. eds. *Education and Capitalism: Struggles for Learning and Liberation*. Chicago: Haymarket.

Jolly, R., Stewart, F., and Cornia, G. A. 1987. *Adjustment with a Human Face*: Clarendon Press; New York.

Juniper, Tony. 2014. "Capitalism v Environment: Can Greed Ever be Green?" (November 26) *The Guardian* https://www.theguardian.com/sustainable-business/2014/nov/26/capitalism-environment-green-greed-slow-life-symposium-tony-juniper

Kahn, Richard. 2010. *Critical Pedagogy, Ecoliteracy & Planetary Crisis: The Ecopedagogy Movement*. NY: Peter Lang.

Kennard, Matt and Claire Provost. 2016. "How Aid Became Big Business,"

Los Angeles Review of Books, May 9. http://pulitzercenter.org/reporting/how-aid-became-big-business

Kincheloe, Joe. 2007. "Critical Pedagogy in the Twenty-First Century: Evolution for Survival." in Peter McLaren, and Joe Kincheloe. eds. *Critical Pedagogy: Where Are We Now?* New York: Peter Lang.

Klees, Steven. forthcoming. "Beyond Neoliberalism: Reflections on Capitalism and Education," *Policy Futures in Education*.

Klees, Steven. 2017. "Will We Achieve Education for All and the Education Sustainable Development Goal?" *Comparative Education Review*, May, 61, 2, 425-40.

Klees, Steven. 2016a. "Human Capital and Rates of Return: Brilliant Ideas or Ideological Dead Ends?" *Comparative Education Review*, 60, no. 4, 644-72.

Klees, Steven. 2016b. "Inferences from Regression Analysis: Are They Valid?" *Real World Economics Review*, April 2016, 74, 85-97.

Klees, Steven. 2016c. "The Political Economy of Education and Inequality: Reflections on Piketty," *Globalisation, Societies and Education*, July, 1-15.

Klees, Steven. 2012. "World Bank and Education: Ideological Premises and Ideological Conclusions," in Klees, Steven, Samoff, Joel, and Nelly Stromquist. eds. *The World Bank and Education: Critiques and Alternatives*. Rotterdam: Sense.

Klees, Steven. 2009. "The Language of Education and Development," in Birgit Brock-Utne and Gunnar Garbo (Eds.) *Language and Power: Implications of Language for Peace and Development*. Ann Arbor: University of Michigan.

Klees, Steven. 2008. "NGOs, Civil Society, and Development: Is There a Third Way?" *Current Issues in Comparative Education*, Spring/Fall, 10 (1&2).

Klees, Steven. 1994. "The Economics of Educational Technology," In T. Husen and T. Neville Postlethwaite. eds. *The International Encyclopedia of Education* (2nd edition). Oxford: Pergamon.

Klees, Steven, Samoff, Joel, and Nelly Stromquist. Eds. 2012. *The World Bank and Education: Critiques and Alternatives*. Rotterdam: Sense.

Klein, Naomi. 2017a. "Daring to Dream in the Age of Trump." *The Nation*,

July 3/10, 15-17.

Klein, Naomi. 2017b. *No is Not Enough. Resisting Trump's Shock Politics and Winning the World We Need*. Chicago: Haymarket.

Klein, Naomi. 2014. *This Changes Everything: Capitalism vs. The Climate*. NY: Simon & Schuster.

Kohn, Alfie. 1988. "Human Nature Isn't Inherently Violent," *Detroit Free Press*, August 21.

Kohn, Alfie. 2000. *The Case Against Standardized Testing: Raising the Scores, Ruining the Schools*. Portsmouth, NH: Heinemann.

Koivusalo Meri. 2009. "The Shaping of Global Health Policy," in Leo Panitch and Colin Leys (eds.) *Morbid Symptoms: Health Under Capitalism*. NY: Monthly Review Press.

Korten, David. 2015. *Change the Story, Change the Future: A Living Economy for a Living Earth*. Oakland, CA: Berrett-Koehler.

Kovel, Joel. 2014. "The Future Will Be Ecosocialist," in Goldin, F., Smith D. and M. Smith (eds.) *Imagine Living in a Socialist USA*. NY: Harper.

Kovel, Joel. 2007. *The Enemy of Nature: The End of Capitalism or the End of the World?* (2nd ed.) NY: Zed.

Krugman, Paul. 2007. *The Conscience of a Liberal*. NY: W. W. Norton.

Krugman, Paul. 2014. "Why We're in a New Gilded Age." *New York Review of Books*, 61, no. 8, 8 May: 15 www.nybooks, com.

Krugman, Paul. 2015. "Slavery's Long Shadow," *New York Times*, June 22. https://mobile.nytimes.com/2015/06/22/opinion/paul-krugman-slaverys-long-shadow.html?mwrsm=Email&_r=0&referrer

Kunkel, Benjamin. 2014. Paupers and Richlings. *London Review of Books* 36, no. 13, July 3: 17-20.

Kuznets, Simon. 1955. "Economic Growth and Income Inequality." *American Economic Review* 45, no. 1: 1-21.

Lakey, George. 2016. *Viking Economics: How the Scandinavians Got It Right – and How We Can, Too*. Brooklyn, NY: Melville House.

Leamer, Edward E. 1983. "Let's Take the Con Out of Econometrics." *American Economic Review* 73 (March): 31-43.

Lesser, Elizabeth. 2016. "How to Talk to People You Disagree With," TED Talk, September 14. https://ed.ted.com/featured/XNDvgIYd

Leys, Colin. 2009. "Health, Health Care and Capitalism," in Leo Panitch and Colin Leys (eds.) *Morbid Symptoms: Health Under Capitalism*. NY: Monthly Review Press.

Lin, Jing. 2006. *Love, Peace, and Wisdom in Education: A Vision for Education in the 21st Century*. NY: Rowman & Littlefield.

Long, Heather. 2017. "Paychecks Hit High for Middle Class," *Washington Post*, September 13, p. A1.

MacLean, Nancy. 2017. *Democracy in Chains: The Deep History of the Radical Right's Stealth Plan for America*. NY: Penguin.

Macpherson, Ian. 2014. "Interrogating the Private School 'Promise' of Low-Fee Private Schools." In Ian Macpherson, Susan Robertson, and Geoffrey Walford. (eds.) *Education, Privatisation and Social Justice*. Oxford; Symposium.

Maher, Bill. 2009. "Health Care Problem Isn't Socialism, It's Capitalism," *Real Clear Politics*, July 24. https://www.realclearpolitics.com/articles/2009/07/24/health_care_problem_isnt_socialism_its_capitalism_97610.html

Malen, B., Croninger, R., Muncey, D. & Jones, D. (2002) "Reconstituting Schools: Testing the Theory of Action, *Education Evaluation and Policy Analysis*, 24, (2), 113-32.

May, Stephen and Christine E. Sleeter. Eds. 2010. *Critical Multiculturalism: Theory and Praxis*. NY: Routledge.

McCowan, Tristan. 2003. "Participation and Education in the Landless People's Movement of Brazil." *Journal for Critical Education Policy Studies* 1 (1). Available at: http://www.jceps.com/?pageID=article&articleID=6

McLaren, Peter. 2000. *Che Guevara, Paulo Freire, and the Pedagogy of Revolution*. Landham, MD: Rowman and Littlefield.

McLaren, Peter. 2007. "The Future of the Past: Reflections on the Present State of Empire and Pedagogy." in Peter McLaren, Peter and Joe Kincheloe. *Critical Pedagogy: Where Are We Now?* New York: Peter Lang.

Meadows, Dennis, Meadows, Donella, Randers, Jergen, and Behrens, William. 1972. *The Limits to Growth*. Rome, Italy: The Club of Rome.

Milanovic, Branko. 2016. *Global Inequality: A New Approach for the Age of Globalization*. Cambridge, MA: Harvard University Press,

Mishel, Lawrence and Schleder, Jessica. 2017. "CEO Pay Remains High Relative to the Pay of Typical Workers and High Wage-Earners," Economic Policy Institute, July 20. http://www.epi.org/publication/ceo-pay-remains-high-relative-to-the-pay-of-typical-workers-and-high-wage-earners/

Motala Enver and Salim Vally. ed. 2014. 'No One to Blame but Themselves:' Rethinking the Relationship between Education, Skills and Employment. In *Education, Economy and Society*. ed. Salim Vally and Enver Motala. Johannesburg: UNISA Press.

Movahed, Masoud. 2016. "Does Capitalism Have to be Bad for the Environment?" (February 15) *World Economic Forum*. https://www.weforum.org/agenda/2016/02/does-capitalism-have-to-be-bad-for-the-environment/

National Commission on Excellence in Education. 1983. *A Nation at Risk: The Imperative of Education Reform*. Washington, DC: US Government Printing Office.

Ne'eman, Ari. 2009. "Disability Politics," *The New Atlantis* (Spring) 24: 112-16.

O'Cadiz, Pilar, Wong, Pia, and Carlos A. Torres. 1998. *Education and Democracy: Paulo Freire, Social Movements, and Educational Reform in Sao Paulo*. Boulder, CO: Westview.

Olmedo, Antonio. 2016. "Philanthropy, Business, and the Changing Roles of Government," Education International, April 4. http://www.unite4education.org/global-response/2813/

Oxfam. 2016. "An Economy for the 1%." Washington, DC: Oxfam. https://www.oxfam.org/sites/www.oxfam.org/files/file_attachments/bp210-economy-one-percent-tax-havens-180116-en_0.pdf

Panitch, Leo and Leys, Colin (eds.) 2007. *Coming to Terms with Nature*. NY: Monthly Review Press.

Panitch, Leo and Leys, Colin (eds.) 2008. *Violence Today: Actually Existing Barbarism*. NY: Monthly Review Press.

Picower, B. 2012. *Practice What You Teach: Social Justice Education in the Classroom and the Streets*. NY: Routledge.

Piketty, Thomas. 2014. *Capital in the Twenty-first Century*. Cambridge, MA;

Harvard University Press.

Pogrow, Stanley. 2017. "The Failure of the US Education Research Establishment to Identify Effective Practices: Beware Effective Practices Policies," *Education Policy Analysis Archives*, 25 (5), 1-19. https://epaa. asu.edu/ojs/article/view/2517

Rakowski, James. 1980. "The Theory of the Second Best and the Competitive Equilibrium Model." *Journal of Economic Issues*, 14: 197-207.

Rand Corporation (n.d.). "Evaluating the Effectiveness of Teacher Pay-for-Performance." Santa Monica, CA: Rand. https://www.rand.org/ capabilities/solutions/evaluating-the-effectiveness-of-teacher-pay-for-performance.html

Rao, Mohan. 2009. "'Health for All' and Neoliberal Globalisation," in Leo Panitch and Colin Leys (eds.) *Morbid Symptoms: Health Under Capitalism*. NY: Monthly Review Press.

Ravitch, Diane. 2013. *Reign of Error: The Hoax of the Privatization Movement and the Danger to America's Public Schools*. NY: Knopf.

Ravitch, Diane. 2010. *The Death and Life of the Great American School System: How Testing and Choice are Undermining Education*. NY: Basic Books.

Reardon, Sean. 2011. "The Widening Academic Achievement Gap Between the Rich and the Poor: New Evidence and Possible Explanations." In Greg J. Duncan and Richard Murnane. eds. *Whither Opportunity? Rising Inequality, Schools, and Children's Life Chances*. NY: Russell Sage Foundation.

Reeves, Richard. 2017. *Dream Hoarders: How the American Upper Middle Class is Leaving Everyone Else in the Dust, Why That is a Problem, and What to Do About It*. Washington, DC: Brookings.

Reich, Robert. 2018. *The Common Good*. NY: Knopf.

Reich, Robert. 2015. *Saving Capitalism*. NY: Knopf.

Reinert, Erik. 2012. "Neoclassical Economics: A Trail of Economic Destruction Since the 1970s," *Real-World Economics Review*, 60, 2-17.

Roosevelt, Franklin D. 1944/n.d. "The Economic Bill of Rights," http:// www.ushistory.org/documents/economic_bill_of_rights.htm

Rothstein, Richard. 2014. "The Colorblind Bind," *American Prospect*. June 22. http://prospect.org/article/race-or-class-future-affirmative-

action-college-campus?utm_source=Economic+Policy+Institute&u
tm_campaign=7e3607c0f2-EPI_News&utm_medium=email&utm_
term=0_e7c5826c50-7e3607c0f2-55907577

Rothstein, Richard. 2017. *The Color of Law: A Forgotten History of How Our Government Segregated America*. NY: Norton.

Roy, Arundhati. 2014. *Capitalism: A Ghost Story*. Chicago: Haymarket.

Russell, Marta and Ravi Malhotra. 2002. "Capitalism and Disability," *Socialist Register*. http://www.socialistregister.com/index.php/srv/article/viewFile/5/84/2680

Saez, Emmanuel and Zucman, Gabriel. Forthcoming. *The Triumph of Injustice*. NY: W.W. Norton.

Sahlberg, Pasi. 2015. *Finish Lessons 2.0: What Can the World Learn from Educational Change in Finland?* NY: Teachers College Press.

Sandbrook, Richard. 2014. *Reinventing the Left in the Global South: The Politics of the Possible*. Cambridge, UK: Cambridge University Press.

Sandel, Michael. 2013. "Why We Shouldn't Trust the Market with our Civic Life," TED talk. https://www.ted.com/talks/michael_sandel_why_we_shouldn_t_trust_markets_with_our_civic_life

Satgar, Vishwas. 2014. *The Solidarity Economy Alternative: Emerging Theory and Practice*. Natal, South Africa: University of KwaZulu-Natal Press.

Schweikart, David. 2002. *After Capitalism*. NY: Rowman and Littlefield.

Shifferd, Kent, Hiller, Patrick and David Swanson. 2015. *A Global Security System: An Alternative to War*. worldbeyondwar.org

Singer, Peter. 2017. "Is Violence the Way to Fight Racism?" *Project Syndicate*. August 23. https://www.project-syndicate.org/commentary/antifa-violence-against-racism-by-peter-singer-2017-08

Smith, Sharon. 2013-14. "Black Feminism and Intersectionality," *International Socialist Review*, No. 91. https://isreview.org/issue/91/black-feminism-and-intersectionality

Sousa Santos, Boaventura de. 2014. *Epistemologies of the South: Justice Against Epistemicide*. Boulder: Paradigm.

Sousa Santos, Boaventura de. 2008. "The World Social Forum and the Global Left." *Politics and Society*, 36 (2): 247-70.

Spring, Joel. 2015. *Economization of Education: Human Capital, Global*

Corporations, Skills-Based Schooling. NY: Routledge.

Stiglitz, Joseph. 2019. "After Neoliberalism." *Project Syndicate*, May 30. https://www.project-syndicate.org/commentary/after-neoliberalism-progressive-capitalism-by-joseph-e-stiglitz-2019-05

Stiglitz, Joseph. 2013. *The Price of Inequality: How Today's Divided Society Endangers Our Future*. NY: Norton.

Swanson, David. 2013. *War No More: The Case for Abolition*. eBookIt.

Syll, Lars Palsson. 2014. "Piketty and the Limits of Marginal Productivity Theory." In *Piketty's Capital in the Twenty-first century*. ed. Edward Fullbrook and Jamie Morgan. UK: College Publications.

Tarlau, Rebecca. 2019. *Occupying Schools, Occupying Land: How the Landless Workers Movement Transformed Brazilian Education*. NY: Oxford University Press.

Tercek, Mark. 2017. "The Biggest Environmental Challenges of 2017," The Nature Conservancy. https://global.nature.org/content/environment2017

The Economist. 2014. A modern Marx. May 3.

Thurow, Lester. 1983. *Dangerous Currents: The State of Economics*. NY: Random House.

Thurow, Lester. 1980. *The Zero-Sum Society: Distribution and the Possibilities for Change*. NY: Basic Books.

United Health Foundation. 2016. "America's Health Rankings: 2016 Annual Report." http://www.americashealthrankings.org/learn/reports/2016-annual-report/comparison-with-other-nations

US Census Bureau. 2012. "Nearly 1 in 5 People have a Disability in the US," https://www.census.gov/newsroom/releases/archives/miscellaneous/cb12-134.html

Verger, Antoni, Fontdevila, Clara, and Zancajo, Adrian. 2016. *The Privatization of Education: A Political Economy of Global Education Reform*. NY: Teachers College.

Wade, Robert H. 2014. "The Piketty Phenomenon and the Future of Inequality." In *Piketty's Capital in the Twenty-first Century*. ed. Edward Fullbrook and Jamie Morgan. UK: College Publications.

Wall, Derek. 2015. *Economics After Capitalism*. London: Pluto.

Wallerstein, Immanuel. 2004. "World-systems Analysis." In G. Modelski (Ed.), *World System History*. Oxford: EOLSS Publishers.

Weiler, Hans. 1984. "The Political Economy of Education and Development." *Prospects*, 19(4):468-77.

West, Cornel. 2005. *Democracy Matters: Winning the Fight Against Imperialism*. NY: Penguin.

Wilkinson, Richard and Pickett, Kate. 2009. *The Spirit Level: Why Greater Equality Makes Societies Stronger*. NY: Bloomsbury.

Wolf, Sherry. 2009. *Sexuality and Socialism: History, Politics, and Theory of LGBT Liberation*. Chicago: Haymarket.

Wolff, Richard. 2012. *Democracy at Work: A Cure for Capitalism*. Chicago: Haymarket.

World Bank. 2001. *Poverty Reduction Strategy*. www.worldbank.org/whatwedo/strategies.htm

World Economic Forum. 2016. "Everybody's Business: Strengthening International Cooperation in a More Interdependent World: Report of the Global Redesign Initiative." http://www3.weforum.org/docs/WEF_GRI_EverybodysBusiness_Report_2010.pdf

World Health Organization. 2017. *World Health Statistics 2017: Monitoring Health for the SDGs*. Geneva: WHO.

Waring, Marilyn. 1988. *If Women Counted: A New Feminist Economics*. NY: Harper & Row.

Wright, Erik O. 2010. *Envisioning Real Utopias*. NY: Verso.

Yancy, George. 2015. "Dear White America," Opinionator, *New York Times*, December 24. https://opinionator.blogs.nytimes.com/2015/12/24/dear-white-america/#more-158804

Yancy, George and hooks, bell. 2015. "bell hooks: Buddhism, the Beats, and Loving Blackness," Opinionator, *New York Times*, December 15. https://opinionator.blogs.nytimes.com/2015/12/10/bell-hooks-buddhism-the-beats-and-loving-blackness/

Yong, Ed. 2016. "Humans: Unusually Murderous Mammals, Typically Murderous Primates," *The Atlantic*, September 28. https://www.theatlantic.com/science/archive/2016/09/humans-are-unusually-violent-mammals-but-averagely-violent-primates/501935/

Zaikowski, C. 2016. "6 Ways Your Social Justice Activism Might Be Ableist," *Everyday Feminism*. http://everydayfeminism.com/2016/09/social-justice-activism-ableist/

Zucman, Gabriel. 2017. *The Hidden Wealth of Nations* (2nd edition). Chicago: University of Chicago Press.

Index

ableism, 8, 14, 114-5, 145
Affordable Care Act (ACA),
    119
Albert, Michael, 88-9, 92
Albritton, Robert, 83
Alexander, Neville, 85
Alperovitz, Gar, 88-9, 92
American Enterprise Institute,
    29, 138
American with Disabilities
    Act (ADA), 115-6
Amin, Samir, 51
Antifa, 132
Apartheid, 85, 106
Apple, Michael, 94
Arab Spring, 91, 156
Aspen Institute, 81
Atkinson, Anthony, 58-9
Au, Wayne, 94
Barash, David, 131
Baxter, Jorge, 98
Bello, Walden, 91
bin Laden, Osama, 134
Black Lives Matter, 104, 106
Bollier, David, 87
Bouveia, Elizabeth, 115
Brazil Landless Movement, 91,
    102, 109, 168
Broad Foundation, 28
buen vivir, 154
Bush, George H. W., 5, 6, 21,
    24
capitalism, 79-93, 145-8
Carnoy, Martin, 10, 41, 47
Cato Institute, 39, 138
chimpanzees, 130
Chomsky, Noam, 91
Citizens United, 57, 82, 150
civil rights movement, 16, 91,
    103, 106, 110
civil society organizations
    (CSOs), 13, 40, 63, 67-70
climate change, 2, 80, 123-7
Clinton, Bill, 111
Clinton Global Initiative, 81
Clinton, Hillary, 6, 111, 143-4
Club of Rome, 154
Coggins, Ross, 75
Coleman Report, 17, 27
colonialism, 85, 104, 107, 115,
    132
Collins, Chuck, 59
communist, 147
compensatory legitimation,
    35, 74
Correa, Rafael, 98
critical pedagogy, 14, 94-7, 100
critical race theory, 97, 100
Cuba, 90, 99, 108-9, 155
Dalit movement, 91, 156
Davis, Angela, 108
de Beauvoir, Simone, 101

de la Fuente, Alejandro, 108-9
Democratic Party, 1, 6, 7
Development Set, The, 75
disabilities, 8, 14, 114-6
Drucker, Peter, 112
East Asian "tigers," 64
Eisenhower, Dwight, 4-5
Economic Policy Institute, 138
economics, 41-51
  efficiency, 12, 13, 42-50, 56-7,
    79-80, 94, 118, 146
  free market system, 7
  GNP, 48-9, 80, 135
  human capital, 41, 60, 83
  macroeconomics, 48
  microeconomics, 43, 48
  market failure, 43-4, 50, 65
  market imperfections, 44
  neoclassical economics, 44-
    50, 55-8, 66, 79-80
  perfect competition, 42-50,
    56, 79
  second best theory, 46
Ecuador, 98, 154
education, 16-40, 94-9
  A Nation at Risk Report, 17,
    23-4
  accountability, 12, 21-4, 37
  achievement gap, 25-7
  Brown v. Board of Education,
    16
  charter schools, 12, 20, 22, 28,
    136
  Citizen School movement, 97

common core, 24-5
critical pedagogy, 14, 94-7,
  100
Education for All (EFA), 33-8,
  70, 73, 121, 149
Fast Track Initiative, 34
Finland, 31
girls' education, 105
Global Partnerhsip for
  Education, 34
Low fee private schools, 37
No Child Left behind
  (NCLB), 21, 25, 30
PISA, 30-1
privatization, 12, 35-8, 94,
  137
Race to the Top, 21, 25
social justice education, 14,
  96
standards, 24-5
teaching, 12, 22-3, 31
testing, 12, 21-5, 28, 30-1, 94
vouchers, 12, 18-21, 135, 137
environment, 7, 8, 12, 14, 45,
  49, 73, 77, 80-3, 86, 88, 92,
  123-8, 141-2, 147, 157
Esteva, Gustavo, 92
ethnicity, 7, 14, 101, 105
feminism, 102-4, 112
Fischer, Joschka, 128
Flake, Jeff, 1, 6
Freire, Paulo, 14, 94-7, 155
Friedman, Milton, 45, 47
Fullbrook, Edward, 50-1

Gandin, Luis, 94
Gates Foundation, 28, 122
gender, 7, 14, 72, 100-5, 112, 115
Giridharadas, Anand, 81
globalization, 13, 71-4, 91, 156
Goldwater, Barry, 1-3, 5, 65
Gorz, Andre, 94
Hahnel, Robin, 88, 92
Guatemala, 67. 105
health, 5, 12, 14, 37, 58, 61, 66, 83, 118-123, 135-7, 150
Heritage Foundation, 39, 138
Hess, Frederick, 29
heterosexism, 8, 14, 100, 108, 145
Holocaust, 115
hooks, bell, 108
Iacocca, Lee, 147
inequality, 4-8, 11, 13, 44-5, 52-9, 80-1, 86, 127
Institute for Policy Studies, 59, 138
International Monetary Fund (IMF), 57-8, 61-3, 71, 122
Japan, 17-8
Jencks, Christopher, 17, 27
Jim Crow Laws, 106
Johnson, Lyndon, 1, 16
Kennard, Matt, 77
Keynes, John Maynard, 48, 87
Klein, Naomi, 125-7, 144-5, 149
Kovel, Joel, 88

Krugman, Paul, 1-8, 55, 92, 106, 108
Kuznets, Simon, 56, 61
Lakey, George, 92
LeGuin, Ursula, 92
Levin, Henry, 10, 41
Leys, Colin, 122
LGBT, 109-13
Lown, Bernard, 133
Lucas, Robert, 56
Maher, Bill, 120, 147
Malhotra, Ravi, 116
market fundamentalism, 13, 80
Marshall Plan, 69, 128, 134
Marx, Karl, 55, 85, 87, 147
Maslow, Abraham, 151
McLaren, Peter, 95,97
Medicaid, 5, 108, 119-20
Medicare, 5, 119-20
Millennium Development Goals (MDGs), 33-7, 72-4
Mondragon Cooperative, 89
Motala, Enver, 85
National Organization of Women, 102, 112
Nazism, 55, 85, 107, 113, 115, 132, 134, 155
New Public Management, 33
nongovernmental organizations (NGOs), 11, 13, 27, 40, 67-9, 77
non-reformist reforms, 94, 97
North Korea, 128-9

nuclear war, 7, 128-9, 133, 142, 147

Obama, Barack, 6, 21-2, 25, 28, 105-6, 111

Obamacare, 119-121

Occupy movement, 53, 91

Oxfam, 77

patriarchy, 7, 8, 57, 103-5, 108, 119, 145

philanthrocapitalists, 28

Pickett, Kate, 58

Piketty, Thomas, 13, 53-6

Provost, Claire, 77

political economy, 45-6, 50-1, 55, 83, 88

poverty, 4, 7, 8, 11, 13, 16, 26-7, 31-2, 44-5, 51-9, 62-3, 68, 72-4, 80. 92, 106, 114, 123, 132, 141, 146-7

poverty reduction strategy (PRS), 62-3, 69

public-private partnerships (PPPs), 76-7, 82

Psacharopoulos, George, 54

racism, 4, 7, 8, 14, 26, 55, 65, 86, 97-8, 100, 103-9, 112, 134, 143-145, 149

Ravitch, Diane, 28-9

Reagan, Ronald, 4, 17, 61

Republican Party, 1, 5, 6, 108

Reeves, Richard, 53

Roosevelt, Franklin D., 6, 157

Russell, Marta, 116

Sanders, Bernie, 1, 7, 92, 143, 148, 156

Sanders, Jane, 92

Santos, Boaventura de Sousa, 91, 154

Save the Children, 77

sexism, 14, 55, 86, 100, 103, 108, 145

Schiavo, Terri, 115

socialism, 7, 55, 87-90, 97-8, 100, 103, 109, 120, 143, 147-8, 150, 153

Sputnik, 18, 24, 30

Stanford University, 9-10, 18, 41, 47, 81

Stiglitz, Joseph, 50, 57-8, 84, 92, 148

Stonewall riots, 110

Structural Adjustment Programs (SAPs), 61-3, 74, 122

Swanson, David, 133-4

Sustainable Development Goals (SDGs), 13, 34-7, 72-7, 153

Syll, Lars, 83, 148

TAPAS, 87, 145

taxes, 5, 27, 39-40, 55, 61, 77, 125-6, 135

Tea Party, 1, 3, 65

Thatcher, Margaret, 61, 85, 145

Thurow, Lester, 50, 55-6

TINA, 85, 87, 145

transgender, 14, 100, 111

Trilateral Commission, 86

Trump, Donald, 3, 6-7, 22, 65, 82, 90, 104, 111, 116, 125, 128-9, 143-4, 155, 157
Ubuntu, 154
Uganda, 113
Un, Kim Jong, 128
UNESCO, 11, 33, 38, 73, 122
UNICEF, 11, 33, 62, 70, 121, 159
United Nations, 33, 72, 77, 82, 116, 152
UNDP, 33, 70
U.S. Agency for International Development (USAID), 11, 77, 105
U.S. Supreme Court, 16, 57, 107, 111, 150
Vally, Salim, 85
Varoufakis, Yanis, 92
Vietnam War, 9, 16
violence, 12, 14, 110, 128-33, 153, 158
Walton Foundation, 28

war, 4, 7-9, 12, 14, 118, 127-34, 142, 147, 158
Washington Consensus, 61-4
West, Cornel, 108
Wikipedia, 89
Wildman, Stephanie, 107
Wilkinson, Richard, 58
Wolf, Sherry, 109
Wolfenson, James, 34
World Bank, 11-12, 33-40, 54, 58, 61-3, 69-71, 84, 122-3, 138
World Economic Forum, 82, 86, 90
World Health Organization (WHO), 121
World Social Forum, 90, 156
World War II, 4, 16, 32, 60
women's movement, 8, 16, 91, 101-5, 110, 156
Wrangham, Richard, 130
Wright, Erik Olin, 86, 88
Zapatistas, 90, 92, 132, 155

CULTURE, SOCIETY & POLITICS

The modern world is at an impasse. Disasters scroll across our smartphone screens and we're invited to like, follow or upvote, but critical thinking is harder and harder to find. Rather than connecting us in common struggle and debate, the internet has sped up and deepened a long-standing process of alienation and atomization. Zer0 Books wants to work against this trend. With critical theory as our jumping off point, we aim to publish books that make our readers uncomfortable. We want to move beyond received opinions.

Zer0 Books is on the left and wants to reinvent the left. We are sick of the injustice, the suffering, and the stupidity that defines both our political and cultural world, and we aim to find a new foundation for a new struggle.

If this book has helped you to clarify an idea, solve a problem or extend your knowledge, you may want to check out our online content as well. Look for Zer0 Books: Advancing Conversations in the iTunes directory and for our Zer0 Books YouTube channel.

Popular videos include:

Žižek and the Double Blackmain

The Intellectual Dark Web is a Bad Sign

Can there be an Anti-SJW Left?

Answering Jordan Peterson on Marxism

Follow us on Facebook
at https://www.facebook.com/ZeroBooks and Twitter at https://twitter.com/Zer0Books

Bestsellers from Zer0 Books include:

Give Them An Argument
Logic for the Left
Ben Burgis
Many serious leftists have learned to distrust talk of logic. This is a serious mistake.
Paperback: 978-1-78904-210-8 ebook: 978-1-78904-211-5

Poor but Sexy
Culture Clashes in Europe East and West
Agata Pyzik
How the East stayed East and the West stayed West.
Paperback: 978-1-78099-394-2 ebook: 978-1-78099-395-9

An Anthropology of Nothing in Particular
Martin Demant Frederiksen
A journey into the social lives of meaninglessness.
Paperback: 978-1-78535-699-5 ebook: 978-1-78535-700-8

In the Dust of This Planet
Horror of Philosophy vol. 1
Eugene Thacker
In the first of a series of three books on the Horror of Philosophy,
In the Dust of This Planet offers the genre of horror as a way of
thinking about the unthinkable.
Paperback: 978-1-84694-676-9 ebook: 978-1-78099-010-1

The End of Oulipo?
An Attempt to Exhaust a Movement
Lauren Elkin, Veronica Esposito
Paperback: 978-1-78099-655-4 ebook: 978-1-78099-656-1

Capitalist Realism
Is There no Alternative?
Mark Fisher
An analysis of the ways in which capitalism has presented itself
as the only realistic political-economic system.
Paperback: 978-1-84694-317-1 ebook: 978-1-78099-734-6

Rebel Rebel
Chris O'Leary
David Bowie: every single song. Everything you want to know,
everything you didn't know.
Paperback: 978-1-78099-244-0 ebook: 978-1-78099-713-1

Kill All Normies
Angela Nagle
Online culture wars from 4chan and Tumblr to Trump.
Paperback: 978-1- 78535-543-1 ebook: 978-1-78535-544-8

Cartographies of the Absolute
Alberto Toscano, Jeff Kinkle
An aesthetics of the economy for the twenty-first century.
Paperback: 978-1-78099-275-4 ebook: 978-1-78279-973-3

Malign Velocities
Accelerationism and Capitalism
Benjamin Noys
Long listed for the Bread and Roses Prize 2015, *Malign Velocities*
argues against the need for speed, tracking acceleration
as the symptom of the ongoing crises of capitalism.
Paperback: 978-1-78279-300-7 ebook: 978-1-78279-299-4

Meat Market
Female Flesh under Capitalism
Laurie Penny
A feminist dissection of women's bodies as the fleshy fulcrum of
capitalist cannibalism, whereby women are both consumers and
consumed.
Paperback: 978-1-84694-521-2 ebook: 978-1-84694-782-7

Babbling Corpse
Vaporwave and the Commodification of Ghosts
Grafton Tanner
Paperback: 978-1-78279-759-3 ebook: 978-1-78279-760-9

New Work New Culture
Work we want and a culture that strengthens us
Frithjoff Bergmann
A serious alternative for mankind and the planet.
Paperback: 978-1-78904-064-7 ebook: 978-1-78904-065-4

Enjoying It
Candy Crush and Capitalism
Alfie Bown
A study of enjoyment and of the enjoyment of studying. Bown
asks what enjoyment says about us and what we say about
enjoyment, and why.
Paperback: 978-1-78535-155-6 ebook: 978-1-78535-156-3

Color, Facture, Art and Design
Iona Singh
This materialist definition of fine-art develops guidelines for
architecture, design, cultural-studies and ultimately social
change.
Paperback: 978-1-78099-629-5 ebook: 978-1-78099-630-1

Neglected or Misunderstood
The Radical Feminism of Shulamith Firestone
Victoria Margree
An interrogation of issues surrounding gender, biology,
sexuality, work and technology, and the ways in which our
imaginations continue to be in thrall to ideologies of maternity
and the nuclear family.
Paperback: 978-1-78535-539-4 ebook: 978-1-78535-540-0

How to Dismantle the NHS in 10 Easy Steps (Second Edition)
Youssef El-Gingihy
The story of how your NHS was sold off and why you will have
to buy private health insurance soon. A new expanded second
edition with chapters on junior doctors' strikes and government
blueprints for US-style healthcare.
Paperback: 978-1-78904-178-1 ebook: 978-1-78904-179-8

Digesting Recipes
The Art of Culinary Notation
Susannah Worth
A recipe is an instruction, the imperative tone of the expert, but
this constraint can offer its own kind of potential. A recipe need
not be a domestic trap but might instead offer escape – something
to fantasise about or aspire to.

Paperback: 978-1-78279-860-6 ebook: 978-1-78279-859-0

Most titles are published in paperback and as an ebook.
Paperbacks are available in traditional bookshops. Both print and
ebook formats are available online.
Follow us on Facebook
at https://www.facebook.com/ZeroBooks
and Twitter at https://twitter.com/Zer0Books